THE BIOCENTRIC WORLDVIEW

Published in the United Kingdom.

ISBN 978-1-907166-61-7

BIC classification:
Social & political philosophy (HPS)

Translation: Joseph D. Pryce
Editor: John B. Morgan
Cover Design: Andreas Nilsson
Layout: Daniel Friberg

Cover illustration: Caspar David Friedrich,
Man and Woman Contemplating the Moon, c. 1824

ARKTOS MEDIA LTD
www.arktos.com

The Biocentric Worldview

Selected Essays and Poems of Ludwig Klages

Translated by Joseph D. Pryce

ARKTOS
London,
2013

Out of Phlegethon!
Out of Phlegethon,
Gerhart
Art thou come forth out of Phlegethon?
with Buxtehude and Klages in your satchel...

— From "Canto LXXV" by Ezra Pound

TABLE OF CONTENTS

"Ludwig Klages is primarily responsible for providing the philosophical foundations for the pan-Romantic conception of man that we now find among many thinkers in different scientific disciplines, for example, Edgar Dacqué, Leo Frobenius, C. G. Jung, Hans Prinzhorn, Theodor Lessing, and, to a certain extent, Oswald Spengler."
— From *Man's Place in Nature* by Max Scheler

"In the field of scientific psychology, Klages towers over all of his contemporaries, including even the academic world's most renowned authorities."
— Oswald Spengler

"*The Spirit as Adversary of the Soul* by Ludwig Klages ranks with Heidegger's *Being and Time* and Hartmann's *The Foundation of Ontology* as one of the three greatest philosophical achievements of the modern epoch."
— Erich Rothacker

"Klages is a fascinating phenomenon, a scientist of the highest rank, whom I regard as the most important psychologist of our time."
— Alfred Kubin

"Ludwig Klages is renowned as the brilliant creator of profound systems of expression-research and graphology, and his new book, entitled *On the Cosmogonic Eros*, possesses such depth of psychological insight and so rich and fructifying an atmosphere, that it moved me far more deeply than I have ever been moved by the writings of men like Spengler and Keyserling. In the pages of this book on the "Cosmogonic Eros," Klages almost seems to have found the very words with which to speak that which has hitherto been considered to be beyond the powers of speech."
— Hermann Hesse

"When we survey the philosophical critiques of Nietzsche's thought that have been published thus far, we conclude that the monograph written by Ludwig Klages, *The Psychological Achievements of Nietzsche*, can only be described as the towering achievement."
— Karl Löwith

On The Biocentric Metaphysics of Ludwig Klages

by Joseph D. Pryce

"Without a doubt, *The Spirit as Adversary of the Soul* by Klages is a great work of philosophy."
— Walter Benjamin

Prelude: The Intellectual Environment

During the closing years of the nineteenth century, the limitations and inadequacies of the superficial positivism that had dominated European thought for so many decades were becoming increasingly apparent to critical observers. The wholesale repudiation of metaphysics that Tyndall, Haeckel and Büchner had proclaimed as a liberation from the superstitions and false doctrines that had misled benighted investigators of earlier times, was now seen as having contributed significantly to the bankruptcy of positivism itself. Ironically, a critical examination of the unacknowledged epistemological assumptions of the positivists clearly revealed that not only had Haeckel and his ilk been unsuccessful in their attempt to free themselves from metaphysical presuppositions, but they had, in effect, merely switched their allegiance from the grand systems of speculative metaphysics that had been constructed in previous eras by the Platonists, Medieval scholastics, and post-Kantian idealists whom they abominated, in order to adhere to a ludicrous, ersatz metaphysics of whose existence they were completely unaware.

The alienation of younger thinkers from what they saw as the discredited dogmas of positivism and materialism found expression in the proliferation of a wide range of philosophical schools, whose adherents had little in common other than the will to revolt against outmoded dogma. "Back to Kant!" became the battle-cry of the neo-Kantians at Marburg. "Back to the things themselves!" proclaimed the "phenomenologist" Edmund Husserl; there were "neo-positivists," "empirio-critical" thinkers, and even the invertebrate American ochlocracy lent its cacophonous warblings to the philosophical choir when William James proclaimed his soothing doctrine of "pragmatism," with which salesmen, journalists, and other uncritical blockheads have stupefied themselves ever since.

A more substantial and significant revolt, however, emerged from another quarter altogether when several independent scholars began to re-examine the speculative metaphysical systems of the "philosophers of nature" who had flourished during the Romantic period. Although the astonishing creativity of these men of genius had been forgotten whilst positivism and materialism ruled the roost, of course, men like Nietzsche, Burckhardt, and Bachofen had preserved elements of the Romantic heritage and had thereby, as it were, already prepared the soil in which younger men would sow the precious seed of a Romantic revival. By the turn of the twentieth century the blossoms had emerged in the form of the philosophers of the "vitalist" school. In France, Henri Bergson became the leading proponent of philosophical vitalism, and his slogan of *élan vital* as well as his doctrine of *évolution créatrice* thrilled audiences in the salons as well as in the university lecture halls. In Hungary, the astonishingly gifted philosopher and physicist, Melchior Palágyi — a thinker of an altogether higher order than the superficial Bergson — conducted profound research into celestial mechanics, which clearly anticipated the theory of relativity; he developed the theory of "virtual" movement; and his critical powers enabled him to craft a definitive and withering refutation of Husserl's pseudo-phenomenology, and his insights retain their validity even now in spite of the oblivion to which the disciples of Husserl have consigned them.

In the German-speaking world the doctrines of *Lebensphilosophie*, or "philosophy of life," achieved academic respectability when Wilhelm Dilthey became their spokesman. Sadly, candor demands that we draw the reader's attention to the troubling fact that it was Dilthey who inaugurated a disastrous trend that was to be maintained at German universities for the next hundred years by such able obfuscators and logomachs as Heidegger and his spawn, for, to put it as charitably as possible, Dilthey was the first significant German philosopher to achieve wide renown in spite of having nothing significant to say (that is why, perhaps, Dilthey and Heidegger furnish such mountains of grist for the philosophical proles who edit and annotate and comment and publish and — *prosper*).

Among these "philosophers of life," there were "amalgamists," among whom we find Hans Driesch, who sabotaged his own project by indulging in futile attempts to combine the irreconcilable doctrines of Kantian idealism and vitalism in his theory of the "entelechy," which, although he proclaimed it to be a uniquely vitalistic notion, is always analyzed mechanistically and atomistically in his expositions. The profound speculative metaphysics of Houston Stewart Chamberlain also succumbed to the Kantian infection, for even Chamberlain seems to have been blind to the ineluctable abyss that divides vitalism and Kantianism.

Finally, and most significantly, we encounter the undisputed master-spirit of the "vitalist" school in the German world, the philosopher and polymath Ludwig Klages, whose system of "biocentric" metaphysics displays a speculative profundity and a logical rigor that no other vitalist on the planet could hope to equal.

THE EARLY YEARS

Ludwig Klages was born on December 10, 1872, in the northern German city of Hannover. He seems to have been a solitary child, but he developed an intense friendship with a class-mate named Theodor Lessing, who would himself go on to achieve fame as the theorist of "Jewish Self-Hatred," a concept whose origins Lessing would later trace back to passionate discussions that he had had with Klages during their boyhood rambles on the windswept moors and beaches of their Lower Saxon home.

In 1891 he received his *Abitur*, and immediately journeyed to Leipzig to begin his university studies in chemistry and physics. In 1893, he moved to Munich, where he would live and work until the Great War forced him into Swiss exile in 1915.

Klages continued his undergraduate studies in Chemistry and Physics during the day, but at night he could usually be found in the cafés of Schwabing, then as now the Bohemian district of Munich. It was in Schwabing that he encountered the poet Stefan George and his circle. George immediately recognized the young man's brilliance, and the poet eagerly solicited contributions from Klages, both in prose and in verse, to his journal, the *Blätter für die Kunst*.

Klages also encountered Alfred Schuler (1865-1923), the profoundly learned Classicist and authority on ancient Roman history, at this time. Schuler was also loosely associated with George's circle, although he was already becoming impatient with the rigidly masculine, "patriarchalist" spirit that seemed to rule the poet and his minions. Klages eventually joined forces with Schuler and Karl Wolfskehl, an authority on Germanistics who taught at the University of Munich, to form the Kosmische Runde, or "Cosmic Circle," and the three young men, who had already come under the influence of the "matriarchalist" anthropology of the late Johann Jakob Bachofen, soon expressed their mounting discontent with George and his "patriarchal" spirit. Finally, in 1904, Klages and Schuler broke with the poet, and the aftermath was one of bitterness and recrimination "all compact." Klages would in later years repudiate his association with George, but he would revere Schuler, both as a man and as a scholar, to the end of his life.

The other crucial experience that Klages had during this last decade of the old century was his overwhelming love affair with Countess Franziska zu Reventlow, the novelist and Bohemian, whose *Notebooks of Mr. Lady* provides what is, perhaps, the most revealing — and comical — rendition of the turbulent events that culminated in the break between the "Cosmic Circle" and the George-Kreis; Wolfskehl, who was himself an eyewitness to the fracas, held that, although Franziska had called the book a novel, it was, in fact, a work of historical fact. Likewise, the diaries of the Countess preserve records of her conversations with Klages (who is referred to as "Hallwig," the name of the Klages surrogate in her "Mr. Lady": she records Klages telling her that "There is no 'God'; *there are many gods!*" At times "Hallwig" even frightens her with oracular allusions to "my mystical side, the rotating Swastika" and with his prophecies of inevitable doom). When the Countess terminated the liaison, Klages, who suffered from serious bouts of major depression throughout his long life, experienced such distress that he briefly contemplated suicide. Fate, of course, would hardly have countenanced such a quietus, for, as Spengler said, there are certain destinies that are utterly inconceivable — Nietzsche won't make a fortune at the gambling tables of Monte Carlo, and Goethe won't break his back falling out of his coach, he remarks drily.

And, we need hardly add, Klages will not die for love...

On the contrary: he will live for *Eros*.

WORKS OF MATURITY

After the epoch-making experiences of the Schwabing years, the philosopher's life seems almost to assume a prosaic, even an anticlimactic, quality. The significant events would henceforth occur primarily in the thinker's inner world and in the publications that communicated the discoveries that he had made therein. There were also continuing commitments on his part to particular institutions and learned societies. In 1903 Klages founded his "Psychodiagnostic Seminars" at the University of Munich, which swiftly became Europe's main center for biocentric psychology. In 1908, he delivered a series of addresses on the application of "expression theory" (*Ausdruckskunde*) to graphological analysis at one such seminar.

In 1910, in addition to the book on expression theory, Klages published the first version of his treatise on psychology, entitled *Prinzipien der Charakterologie* (Principles of Characterology). This treatise was based upon lectures that Klages had delivered during the previous decade, and in its pages he announced his discovery of the "Id," which has popularly, and hence erroneously, for so long been attributed to Freud. He came in personal contact with several members of rival psychological schools during this period, and he was even invited — in his capacity as Europe's leading exponent of graphology — to deliver a lecture on the "Psychology of Handwriting" to the Wednesday night meeting of the Freudian "Vienna Society" on October 25, 1911.

The philosopher also encountered the novelist Robert Musil, in whose masterpiece, *Der Mann ohne Eigenschaften* (The Man Without Qualities), Klages appears — in caricatured form, of course — as the eerie and portentous prophet Meingast, that "messenger from Zarathustra's mountain." The novelist seems to have been most impressed by the philosopher's speculations in *Vom kosmogonischen Eros* (On the Cosmogonic Eros) concerning the ecstatic nature of the "erotic rapture" and the Klagesian "other condition" (*andere Zustand*). Paradoxically, however, Musil's novel presents Meingast (Klages) as a manic and domineering worshiper of power, which is quite strange when one considers that Klages consistently portrays the Nietzschean "will to power" as nothing but a modality of hysteria perfectly appropriate to our murderous age of militarism and capitalism. Anyone familiar with the withering onslaught against the will and its works which constitutes the section entitled "Die Lehre der Wille" in Klages' *Der Geist als Widersacher der Seele* too much importance to them. Reality is composed of images (*Bilder*) and not feelings, and the most important idea that Klages ever developed is his conception of the "actuality of the images" (*Wirklichkeit der Bilder*). He also savages the insane asceticism of Christianity, arguing that a satisfied sexuality is essential for all genuine cosmic radiance. Christ is to be detested as the herald of the annihilation of the Earth and the mechanization of man.

The pioneering treatise on "expression theory," the *Ausdruckskunde und Gestaltungskraft* (Expression Analysis and Formative Force), also appeared in 1913. The first part of his treatise on the interpretation of dreams (*Vom Traumbewusstsein*) appeared in 1914, but war soon erupted in Europe, swiftly interrupting all talk of dreams. Sickened by the militaristic insanity of the "Great War," Klages moved to neutral Switzerland. In 1920 he made his last move to Kilchberg, near Zurich, Switzerland, where he would spend the rest of his life.

The first substantial excerpt from the treatise that would eventually become his *Hauptwerk, Der Geist als Widersacher der Seele*, was published as *Geist und Seele* in a 1916 issue of the journal *Deutsche Psychologie*. He soon turned his attention to the more mundane matter of the contemporary world situation, and in 1918, concerned by the spread of "One World"-humanitarianism and other pernicious forms of "humanism," Klages published the classic *Brief über Ethik* (Letter on Ethics), in which he re-emphasized his opposition to all ethical and individualistic attempts to improve the world. The modern world's increasing miscegenation has hatched out a horde of mongrels, slaves, and criminals. The world is falling under the dominion of the enemies of life, and it matters not a bit whether the ethical fanatic dubs his hobbyhorse *Wille, Tat, Logos, Nous, Idee, Gott*, the "Supreme Being," *reines Subjekt*, or *absolutes Ich*: these phrases are merely fronts behind which spirit, the eternal adversary of life, conducts her nefarious operations. Only infrahuman nature, wherein dwells a principle of hierarchical order in true accord with the laws of life, is able to furnish man with genuine values. The preachers of morality can only murder life with their prohibitive commands so stifling to the soul's vitality. As Klages' disciple Hans Prinzhorn cautions us, the vital order "must not be falsified, according to the Judæo-Christian outlook, into a principle of purposefulness, morality, or sentimentality." The *Letter on Ethics* urges us to avoid all such life-hostile values, and to prize instead those moments when we allow our souls to find warmth in the love which manifests itself as adoration, reverence, and admiration. The soul's true symbol is the mother with her beloved child, and the soul's true examples are the lives of poets, heroes, and gods. Klages concludes his sardonic *Letter* by informing the reader, in contemptuous and ironical tones, that if he refuses to respond to these exemplary heroes, he may then find it more congenial to sit himself down and listen, unharmed, to a lecture on ethics!

In 1921, Klages published his *Vom Wesen des Bewusstseins* (On the Nature of Consciousness), an investigation into the nature of consciousness, in which the ego-concept is shown to be neither a phenomenon of pure spirit nor of pure life, but rather a mere epiphenomenal precipitate of the warfare between life and spirit. In this area, Klages' presentation invites comparison with the Kantian exposition of "pure subjectivity," although, as one might expect, Klages assails the subjectivity of the ego as a hollow sham. The drive to maximize the realm of ego, regardless of whether this impulse clothes itself in such august titles as "the will to power" (Nietzsche), the "will to live" (Schopenhauer), or the naked obsession with the "ego and its own" (Stirner), is merely a manifestation of malevolent *Geist*. Klages also ridicules the superficiality of William James' famous theory of "stream of consciousness," which is subjected to a withering critical onslaught. After James' "stream" is conclusively demolished, Klages demonstrates that Melchior Palágyi's theory more profoundly analyzes the processes whereby we receive the data of consciousness. Klages endorses Palágyi's account of consciousness in order to establish the purely illusory status of the "stream" by proving conclusively that man receives the "images" as discrete, rhythmically pulsating "intermittencies."

We should say a few words about the philosopher whose exposition of the doctrine of consciousness so impressed Klages. Melchior Palágyi (1859-1924) was the Hungarian-Jewish *Naturphilosoph* who was regarded as something of a mentor by the younger man, ever since 1908, when they first met at a learned conference. Like Klages, Palágyi was completely devoted to the thought-world of German Romantic *Naturphilosophie*. Klages relied heavily on this thinker's expert advice, especially with regard to questions involving mechanics and physics, upon which the older man had published outstanding technical treatises. The two men had spent many blissful days together in endless metaphysical dialogue when Palágyi visited Klages at his Swiss home shortly before Palágyi's death. They were delighted with each other's company, and reveled even in the cut and thrust of intense exchanges upon matters about which they were in sharp disagreement. Although this great thinker is hardly recalled today even by compilers of "comprehensive" encyclopedias, Palagyi's definitive and irrefutable demolition of Edmund Husserl's spurious system of "phenomenology" remains one of the most lethal examples of philosophical *adversaria* to be found in the literature. Palágyi, who was a Jew, had such a high opinion of his anti-Semitic colleague, that when Palágyi died in 1925, one of the provisions of his will stipulated that Ludwig Klages was to be appointed as executor and editor of Palágyi's posthumous works, a task that Klages undertook scrupulously and reverently, in spite of the fact that the amount of labor that would be required of him before the manuscripts of his deceased colleague could be readied for publication would severely disrupt his own work upon several texts, most especially the final push to complete the three-volume *Der Geist als Widersacher der Seele*. One gets the impression that Klages felt the task that had been imposed upon him was also one of the highest honors, and Klages' high regard for Palágyi's thought can best be appreciated when we realize that among the numerous thinkers and scholars whose works are cited in his collected works, the contemporary philosopher who is cited most frequently, and at the greatest length, is none other than Melchior Palágyi.

Klages published his influential anthropological-historical study, *Vom kosmogonischen Eros*, in 1922, and in the *Selbstbericht* (Self-critique) which serves as an introduction to this work he details the points of agreement and disagreement between his views and those of Friedrich Nietzsche.

In 1923 Klages published his *Vom Wesen des Rhythmus* (On the Nature of the Rhythmic — a revised edition of which would be issued in 1934). Then in 1925, two fervent admirers of Klagesian biocentrism — one was Niels Kampmann who would go on to publish some of Klages' works in book form — brought out the first issue of a scholarly journal, the brilliant *Zeitschrift für Menschenkunde* (The Journal of Anthropology), which would continue to publish regularly until the rigors of war eventually forced the editors to suspend publication in 1943 (eight years after the end of the war, the journal began a new career in 1953).

A revised and enlarged edition of the treatise on characterology appeared in 1926 with the new title *Die Grundlagen der Charakterkunde* (The Foundations of Characterology). Klages also published *Die psychologischen Errungenschaften Nietzsches* (The Psychological Achievements of Nietzsche) in this same year, a work which, more than a quarter of a century after its initial appearance, the Princeton-based Nietzsche scholar Walter Kaufmann — surely no friend to Klages! — would nevertheless admire greatly, even feeling compelled to describe Klages' exegesis of Nietzsche's psychology as "the best monograph" ever written on its subject.

A collection of brief essays entitled *Zur Ausdruckslehre und Charakterkunde* (On the Theory of Expression and Characterology), was brought out by Kampmann in 1927; many of them date from the early days of the century and their sheer profundity and variety reinforce our conviction that Klages was a mature thinker even in his twenties.

The first two volumes of his magnum opus, the long-awaited and longer-pondered, *Der Geist als Widersacher der Seele*, finally appeared in 1929. One year later the *Graphologisches Lesebuch* (Textbook on Graphology) appeared, and the third and final volume of *Der Geist* hit the book-shops in 1932, a year that seems to have been a very busy one indeed for our polymathic philosopher, since he also found time to revamp his slender monograph entitled *Goethe als Naturforscher* (Goethe as a Scientist), a short work that can only be compared to the books about Goethe by H. S. Chamberlain and Friedrich Gundolf for breadth of scholarship and insight into the creativity of a great seer and scientist (this study was a revised edition of a lecture that had originally been published in the *Jahrbuch des Freien Deutschen Hochstifts* in 1928).

Hans Prinzhorn, the psychologist, translator of D. H. Lawrence and compiler of the landmark treatise on art produced by the mentally disturbed, had long been a friend and admirer of Klages, and in 1932 he organized the celebration for the sixtieth birthday of the philosopher. The tributes composed the various scholars who participated in this event were collected and edited by Prinzhorn for publication in book form, with the title *Festschrift zum 60. Geburtstag.*

NATIONAL SOCIALIST GERMANY, WORLD WAR II, AND THEIR AFTERMATH

Shortly after the National Socialist German Workers' Party (NSDAP) assumed power at the beginning of 1933, one of Klages' disciples established the Arbeitskreises für biozentrisches Forschung (Workgroup for Biocentric Research). At first the German disciples of Klages were tolerated as harmless philosophical eccentrics, but soon the Gestapo began keeping a close eye on members and contributors to the biocentric circle's house organ *Janus*. By 1936 the authorities forcibly shut down the journal and from that time until the fall of the regime, the Gestapo would periodically arrest and question those who had been prominent members of the now-defunct "circle." From 1938 onwards, when Reichsleiter Dr. Alfred Rosenberg delivered a bitter attack on Klages and his school in his inaugural address to the summer semester at the University of Halle, the official party spokesmen explicitly and repeatedly condemned Klages and his friends as enemies of the National Socialist worldview.

Klages traveled widely during the 1930s, and he especially enjoyed his journeys to Greece and Scandinavia. In 1940 he published *Alfred Schuler, Fragmente und Vorträge: Aus dem Nachlass* (Alfred Schuler, Fragments and Lectures: From the Notebooks), his edition of Alfred Schuler's literary remains. The Introduction to the anthology is a voluminous critical memoir in which Klages rendered profound tribute to his late mentor. However, in the pages of that introduction, Klages introduced several statements critical of "World-Jewry" that were to dog his steps for the rest of his life, just as they have compromised his reputation after his death. Unlike so many *ci-devant* "anti-Semites" who prudently saw the philo-Semitic light in the aftermath of the war, however, Klages scorned to repudiate anything that he had said on this or any other topic. He even poured petrol on the fires by voicing his conviction that the only significant difference between the species of master-race nonsense that was espoused by the National Socialists and the variety adopted by their Jewish enemies was in the matter of results: Klages blandly proclaims that the Jews, after a two-thousand-year-long assault on the world for which they felt nothing but hatred, had actually won the definitive victory. There would be no re-match. He sneered at all the kow-towing to Jewry that had already become part of the game in the immediate post-war era, because, he reasoned, even as a tactical ploy, such sycophantic behavior has always doomed itself to complete and abject failure.

In December of 1942, the official daily newspaper of the NSDAP, the *Völkischer Beobachter*, published a vicious and ungracious attack on Klages in the edition that appeared on the philosopher's seventieth birthday. During the war years, Klages began compiling notes for a projected full-dress autobiography that was, sadly, never completed. Still, the notes are fascinating in their own right, and are well worth consulting by the student of his life and thought.

In 1944, Barth of Leipzig published the *Rhythmen und Runen* (Rhythms and Runes), a self-edited anthology of Klages' prose and verse writings stemming from the turn of the century (unfortunately, however, when Bouvier finally brought out their edition of his "Collected Works," which began to appear in the mid-1960s, *Rhythmen und Runen*, along with the monograph on Stefan George and such provocative pieces as the Introduction to Schuler's writings, were omitted from the set, in spite of the fact that the original prospectus issued to subscribers announced that these works would, in fact, be included. The reasons for this behavior are — need we say? — quite obvious).

When the war ended, Klages began to face true financial hardship, for his market, as well as his publishers, had been devastated by the horrific saturation bombing campaign with which the democratic allies had turned Germany into a shattered and burnt-out wasteland. Klages also suffered dreadfully when he learned that his beloved sister, Helene, as well as her daughter Heidi, the philosopher's niece, had perished in the agony of post-war Germany. Although Klages had sought permission from the occupying authorities to visit his sister as she lay dying, his request was ignored. This refusal, followed shortly by his receipt of the news of her miserable death, aroused an almost unendurable grief in his soul.

His spirits were raised somewhat by the *Festschrift* that was organized for his 80th birthday, and his creative drive certainly seemed to have remained undiminished by the ravages of advancing years. He was deeply immersed in the philological studies that prepared him to undertake his last great literary work, *Die Sprache als Quell der Seelenkunde* (Language as Source of Psychology), which was published in 1948. In this dazzling monument of twentieth century scholarship, Klages conducted a comprehensive investigation of the relationship between psychology and linguistics. During that same year he also directed a devastating broadside in which he refuted the fallacious doctrines of Jamesian "pragmatism" as well as the infantile sophistries of Watson's "behaviorism." This brief but pregnant essay was entitled "Wie Finden Wir die Seele des Nebenmenschen?"

During the early 1950s, Klages' health finally began to deteriorate, but he was at least heartened by the news that there were serious plans afoot among his admirers and disciples to get his classic treatises back into print as soon as possible. Death came at last to Ludwig Klages on July 29, 1956. The cause of death was determined to have been a heart attack. He is buried in the Kilchberg cemetery, which overlooks Lake Zurich.

UNDERSTANDING KLAGESIAN TERMS

A brief discussion of the philosopher's technical terminology may provide the best preparation for an examination of his metaphysics. Strangely enough, the relationship between two familiar substantives, "spirit" (*Geist*) and "soul" (*Seele*), constitutes the main source of our terminological difficulties. Confusion regarding the meaning and function of these words, especially when they are employed as technical terms in philosophical discourse, is perhaps unavoidable at the outset. We must first recognize the major problems involved before we can hope to achieve the necessary measure of clarity. Klages regards the study of semantics, especially in its historical dimension, as our richest source of knowledge regarding the nature of the world (metaphysics, or philosophy) and an unrivalled tool with which to probe the mysteries of the human soul (psychology, or characterology [*Charakterkunde*]). We would be well advised, therefore, to adopt an extraordinary stringency in lexical affairs. We have seen that the first, and in many ways the greatest, difficulty that can impede our understanding of biocentric thought confronts us in our dealings with the German word *Geist*. *Geist* has often been translated as "spirit" or "mind," and, less often, as "intellect." As it happens, the translation of Hegel's *Phänomenologie des Geistes* that most American students utilized in their course-work during the 1960s and 1970s was entitled *The Phenomenology of Mind* (G. W. F. Hegel, *The Phenomenology of Mind* [New York: Harper Torchbooks, 1967], translated by J. B. Bailey).

Lest it be thought that we are perversely attributing to the word *Geist* an exaggeratedly polysemic status, we would draw the reader's attention to the startling fact that Rudolf Hildebrandt's entry on this word in the Grimm *Wörterbuch* comprises more than one hundred closely printed columns. Hildebrandt's article has even been published separately as a book. Today in everyday English usage, spirit (along with its cognates) and soul (along with its cognates) are employed as synonyms. As a result of the lexical habits to which we have grown accustomed, our initial exposure to a philosopher who employs soul and spirit as *antonyms* can be a somewhat perplexing experience. It is important for us to realize that we are not entering any quixotic protest here against familiar lexical custom. We merely wish to advise the reader that whilst we are involved in the interpretation of Klagesian thought, soul and spirit are to be treated consistently as technical philosophical terms bearing the specific meanings that Klages has assigned to them.

Our philosopher is not being needlessly obscure or perversely *recherché* in this matter, for although there are no unambiguous distinctions drawn between soul and spirit in English usage, the German language recognizes some very clear differences between the terms *Seele* and *Geist*, and Hildebrandt's article amply documents the widely ramified implications of the distinctions in question. In fact, literary discourse in the German-speaking world is often characterized by a lively awareness of these very distinctions. Rudolf Kassner, for instance, tells us that his friend, the poet Rainer Maria Rilke, inhabited a world of soul (*Seele*), not one of spirit (*Geist*). In speaking of Rilke's world as that of the soul, Kassner is proclaiming the indisputable truth that Rilke's imagination inhabits an innocent, or pagan, world, a realm that is utterly devoid of such "spiritual" baggage as "sin" and "guilt." Likewise, for Kassner, as for Rilke, the world of spirit is the realm of labor and duty, which is ruled by abstractions and "ideals." I can hardly exaggerate the significance of the spirit-soul dichotomy upon which Kassner has shed so much light in these remarks on Rilke as the man of "soul." If the reader bears their substance in mind, he will find that the path to understanding shall have been appreciably cleared of irksome obstacles.

Therefore, these indispensable lexical distinctions are henceforth to function as our established linguistic protocol. Bearing that in mind, when the reader encounters the Klagesian thesis which holds that man is the battlefield on which soul and spirit wage a war to the death, even the novice will grasp some portion of the truth that is being enunciated. And the initiate who has immersed his whole being in the biocentric doctrine will swiftly discover that he is very well prepared indeed to perpend, for instance, the characterological claim that one can situate any individual at a particular point on an extensive typological continuum at one extreme of which we situate such enemies of sexuality and sensuous joy as the early Christian hermits or the technocrats and militarists of our own day, all of whom represent the complete dominance of *spirit*; and at the opposite extreme of which we locate the Dionysian maenads of Antiquity and those rare modern individuals whose delight in the joys of the senses enables them to attain the loftiest imaginable pinnacle of ecstatic vitality: the members of this second group, of course, comprise *the party of life*, whose ultimate allegiance is rendered to *soul*.

Before we conclude this brief digression into terminological affairs, we would advise those readers whose insuperable hostility to every form of metaphysical "idealism" compels them to resist all attempts to "place" spirit and soul as "transcendental" entities, that they may nevertheless employ our terms as heuristic expedients, much as Ampére employed the metaphor of the "swimmer" in the electric "current."

BIOCENTRIC METAPHYSICS IN ITS HISTORICAL CONTEXT

Perhaps a brief summary will convey at least some notion of the sheer originality and the vast scope of the biocentric metaphysics. Let us begin by placing some aspects of this philosophical system in historical context. For thousands of years, Western philosophers have been deeply influenced by the doctrine, first formulated by the Eleatic School and Plato, which holds that the images that fall upon our sensorium are merely deceitful phantoms. Even those philosophers who have rebelled against the schemes devised by Plato and his successors, and who consider themselves to be "materialists," "monists," "logical atomists," and so on, reveal that they have been infected by the disease even as they resist its onslaught, for in many of their expositions the properties of matter are presented as if they were independent entities floating in a void that suspiciously resembles the transcendent Platonic realm of the "forms."

Ludwig Klages, on the other hand, demonstrates that it is precisely the images and their ceaseless transformations that constitute the only realities. In the unique phenomenology of Ludwig Klages, images constitute the souls of such phenomena as plants, animals, human beings, and even the cosmos itself. These images do not deceive: they *express*; these living images are not to be "grasped," not to be rigidified into concepts: they are to be *experienced*. The world of things, on the other hand, forms the proper subject of scientific explanatory schemes that seek to "fix" things in the "grasp" of concepts. Things are appropriated by men who owe their allegiance to the will and its projects. The agents of the will appropriate the substance of the living world in order to convert it into the dead world of things, which are reduced to the status of the material components required for purposeful activities such as the industrial production of high-tech weapons systems. This purposeful activity manifests the outward operations of an occult and daemonic principle of destruction.

Klages calls this destructive principle "spirit" (*Geist*), and he draws upon the teaching of Aristotle in attempting to account for its provenance, for it was Aristotle who first asserted that spirit (*nous*) invaded the substance of man from "outside." Klages' interpretation of this Aristotelian doctrine leads him to conclude that spirit invaded the realm of life from outside the spatio-temporal world. Likewise, Klages draws on the thought of Duns Scotus, Occam and other late Medieval English thinkers when he situates the characteristic activity of spirit in the *will* rather than in the intellect. Completely original, however, is the Klagesian doctrine of the mortal hostility that exists between spirit and life (soul). The very title of the philosopher's major metaphysical treatise proclaims its subject to be *The Spirit as Adversary of the Soul*.

The indivisible body-soul unity that had constituted the living substance of man during the "primordial," or prehistoric, phase of his existence, in time becomes the focus of spirit's war against life. Spirit severs the vital connection by thrusting itself, like the thin end of an invasive wedge, between the poles of body and soul. History is the tragic chronicle that recounts the ceaseless war that is waged by spirit against life and soul. When the ever-expanding breach between body and soul finally becomes an unbridgeable abyss, the living substance is no more, although no man can predict how long man may endure as a hollow shell or simulacrum. The ceaseless accumulation of destructive power by spirit is accompanied by the reduction of a now devitalized man to the status of a mere machine, or "robot," who soullessly regurgitates the hollow slogans about "progress," "democracy," and the delights of "the consumer society" that are the only values recognized in this world of death. The natural world itself becomes mere raw material to be converted into "goods" for the happy consumer.

AN AGE OF CHAOS

In the biocentric phenomenology of Ludwig Klages, the triadic historical development of human consciousness, from the reign of life, through that of thought, to the ultimate empire of the raging will, is reflected in the mythic-symbolic physiognomy which finds expression in the three-stage, "triadic," evolution from "Pelasgian" man — of the upper Neolithic and Bronze Ages of pre-history; through the Promethean — down to the Renaissance; to the Heracleic man — the terminal phase that we now occupy, the age to which two brilliant twentieth century philosophers of history, Julius Evola and Savitri Devi, have applied the name "Kali Yuga," which in Hinduism and Buddhism is the dark age of chaos and violence that precedes the inauguration of a new "Golden Age," when a fresh cycle of cosmic events dawns in bliss and beauty.

And it is at this perilous juncture that courageous souls must stiffen their sinews and summon up their blood in order to endure the doom that is closing before us like a mailed fist. Readers may find some consolation, however, in our philosopher's expressions of agnosticism regarding the ultimate destiny of man and Earth. Those who confidently predict the end of all life and the ultimate doom of the cosmos are mere swindlers, Klages assures us. Those who cannot successfully predict such mundane trivialities as next season's fashions in hemlines or the trends in popular music five years down the road can hardly expect to be taken seriously as prophets who can foretell the ultimate fate of the entire universe!

In the end, Ludwig Klages insists that we must never underestimate the resilience of life, for we have no yardstick with which to measure the magnitude of life's recuperative powers. "All things are in flux." That is all.

"Oliveira said, 'Let's keep on looking for the Yonder, there are plenty of Yonders that keep opening up one after the other. I'd start by saying that this technological reality that men of science and the readers of France-Soir accept today, this world of cortisone, gamma rays, and plutonium, has as little to do with reality as the world of the Roman de la Rose. If I mentioned it a while back to our friend Perico, it was in order to make him take note that his æsthetic criteria and his scale of values are pretty well liquidated and that man, after having expected everything from intelligence and from the spirit, feels that he's been betrayed, is vaguely aware that his weapons have been turned against him, that culture and civiltà, have misled him into this blind alley where scientific barbarism is nothing but a very understandable reaction. Please excuse my vocabulary.' 'Klages has already said all of that,' said Gregorovius."

— From Chapter 99 of *Hopscotch* by Julio Cortázar

Editor's Note

Most of the texts included in this volume were translated from the *Sämtliche Werke* (Collected Works) of Klages, which was published in 15 volumes by H. Bouvier of Bonn between 1964 and 1978. Specific citations are as follows:

- "Man and Earth": "Mensch und Erde," vol. 3: pp. 614-630
- "On Ethics": "Brief über Ethik," vol. 3: pp. 664-673
- "On Truth and Actuality": "Über Wahrheit und Wirklichkeit," vol. 3, pp. 720-723
- "On the Problem of Socrates": "Das Problem der Sokrates," vol. 3, pp. 656-663
- "On Consciousness and Life": "Bewusstsein und Leben," vol. 3, pp. 646-655
- "Carl Gustav Carus as Romantic Thinker": excerpt from "Stammväter der Seelenkunde" ("The Founding Fathers of Psychology"), vol. 4, pp. 573-578
- "On the Value of Science": "Vom Wert der Wissenschaft," vol. 3, pp. 710-714
- "Nature vs. Nurture": Excerpt from "Vom Verhältnis der Erziehung zum Wesen des Menschen" ("On the Relationship between Education and the Nature of Man"), vol. 3, pp. 729-730
- "The Problems of Psychology": "Probleme der Seelenkunde," vol. 4, pp. 696-700
- "Goethe as Psychologist": "Goethe als Seelenforscher," vol. 4, pp. 564-568
- "On Love as *Eros* and as Passion": "Schlusswort über *Eros* und Leidenschaft" (final chapter of *Vom kosmogonischen Eros*), vol. 3, pp. 471-473

24

- "The Identity of Spirit in Every Bearer of Life": "Die Einerleiheit des Geistes in allen Bewusstseinsträgern," vol. 3, pp. 334-336

The original year of publication is given at the head of each essay.

"On 'Psychoanalysis'" and "On Academic Psychology and Characterology" were both taken from *Die Grundlagen der Charakterkunde*, originally published in 1928. These translations were also made from the *Sämtliche Werke*, vol. 4. pp. 191-428.

All of the poems were selected from the volume *Rythmen und Runen* that was published by Johann Ambrosius Barth of Leipzig in 1944, although the poems themselves were originally composed at the turn of the twentieth century.

I would like to thank Joe Pryce, who very possibly possesses the most cultivated literary mind I have ever encountered, for giving Arktos the opportunity to publish these translations of an unjustly neglected thinker of the modern German tradition.

JOHN B. MORGAN
Panjim, Goa, India
February 2013

Man and Earth (1913)

Every age, and ours is surely no exception, proclaims certain slogans that embody the inner tendencies of the age. Such slogans possess the power to silence the voice of doubt in the minds of disciples as if with a deafening roar of drums. A new trend is always on display, and even the unbiased few soon congregate around its banner. The three predominant slogans of our own time are "progress," "culture," and "personality." As it happens, in order that the idea of progress may achieve ascendancy as the exclusive creed of our times, its rivals soon relinquish their positions and lend their support, and even their characteristic colors, to the victor. Thus, there are those who suggest that we cannot be inferior to the "primitive" peoples to whom our history books devote a few preliminary paragraphs, and for anyone who questions them as to the basis for their conviction, they have a ready response: science now commands heights never before achieved, and technology has at last subjugated nature — *therefore*, every earlier form of human culture must beat a helpless retreat before them. Science, which now effectively exploits the inexhaustible riches of the Earth, methodically contributes to the general prosperity; space and time are permeated by long-distance communication systems, and even the limitless atmosphere has finally been "conquered" by the genius of technology. It is not, however, for the convinced disciple of this faith in technology (which will die with him), but more for the members of a younger generation, which still asks questions, that we desire to lift at least a corner of the veil in order to reveal the perilous self-deception that lurks behind it.

In addition, those who still see something strange in the view that the guiding idea of "progress" has led to horrendous results, should be puzzled for other reasons. To the ancient Greeks, the loftiest desire was to achieve *kalokagathie*, which was that harmonious wedding of man's inner and outer beauty that they saw embodied in the images of the Olympians; to the men of the Middle Ages, it was the "salvation of the soul," which they saw as the soul's ultimate ascension to God; to the man of Goethe's time, it was the poised perfection of style, the masterful acceptance of one's destiny; and no matter how diverse such goals may have been, we can easily comprehend the profound satisfaction that was experienced by those whose good fortune enabled them to achieve them. But the progress-monger of today is *mindlessly* proud of his successes, for he has somehow managed to convince himself that every increase in mankind's power entails an equivalent increase in mankind's *value*. We must doubt, however, whether he is able to experience true joy, and not just the hollow satisfaction afforded him by the mere possession of power. By itself, however, power is completely blind to all values, blind to truth as it is blind to justice. Finally, power is undoubtedly blind to all the beauty of the life that has thus far survived the encounter with "progress." Let us add some well-known items to our account.

The pre-eminence of science is conceded; it is immune to all objections, however slight. The high standing of technology is also beyond doubt. And yet one might well ask: what are its fruits? As the Bible wisely says, it is only "by their fruits" that we should estimate the value of the works of man. Let us begin with beings whose status as living organisms no one would question: the plants and animals. We recall that the ancients dreamt of a lost "Golden Age," or "paradise," a realm wherein the lion would lie down with the lamb, and the serpent would dwell with man as his protective spirit. Even this idea is not so utterly fantastic as the false doctrine that teaches us that all of nature is perpetually in the grip of a ceaseless "struggle for existence."

The scientists who study the polar regions tell us of the fearless intimacy with which penguins, reindeers, sea lions, seals, and sea-gulls greet the first appearance of man. Pioneers who have explored the tropical regions never fail to amaze us with the images they communicate, especially those which pertain to the moment in which these students first perceive, arrayed in peaceful cohabitation, swarms of wild geese, cranes, ibis, flamingoes, herons, storks, marabous, giraffes, zebras, gnus, antelopes, and gazelles. We understand completely the true symbiosis that embraces the entire animal kingdom, and which extends throughout the entire planet. However, as soon as the man of "progress" arrives on the scene, he announces his masterful presence by spreading death and the horror of death all around him. How many of the species of creatures that flourished in ancient Germanic lands have lasted into our century? Bear and wolf, lynx and wildcat, bison, elk and aurochs, eagle and vulture, crane and falcon, swan and owl, have all become creatures inhabiting only our fairy-tales; this was the case, in fact, even before the introduction of our new and improved wars of annihilation. But there is cause for even deeper merriment. Under the most moronic of all pretexts — which insists that vast numbers of animal species are actually noxious pests — our progress-monger has extirpated nearly every creature who happens not to be a partridge, a roe-deer, a pheasant, or, if need be, a pig. Wild boar, ibex, fox, pine marten, weasel, duck and otter — all animals with which the legends dear to our memory are intimately intertwined — are shrinking in numbers, where, that is, they have not already become extinct; sea gull, tern, cormorant, duck, heron, kingfisher, red kite and owlet are all ruthlessly hunted down; the communities of seals on the coasts of the North Sea and the Baltic are condemned to destruction. We know more than two hundred names of German towns and villages whose names derive from the word "beaver," a fact that constitutes proof of the flourishing of these industrious rodents in earlier times; today there still exists a small preserve on the Elbe river between Torgau and Wittenberg, but even this refuge will soon disappear without immediate statutory protection. And who is not afflicted with grave anxiety to witness, year after year, the disappearance of our beloved singers, the migratory birds? Only a mere generation ago the blue air of our cities was filled all summer long with the whir and buzz of swallows and the cries of sailors, sounds that, emerging from the distance, seemed to fill one with the yearning for travel. At that time, one could count, in one suburb of Munich alone, as many as three hundred occupied nests, whereas today one can only find four or five. More ominously, the countryside has become eerily silent, throbbing no longer as it once did every dew-laden morning in the joyous melody of Eichendorff's "countless larks." Already one must consider oneself fortunate if, whilst walking along a remote forest path near a grassy, sunlit hollow, one is privileged to hear just once the luminous and yearning call of the quail; at one time, throughout the length and breadth of Germany, these birds numbered many, many thousands, and they lived in the songs of the common people as well as in the works of our poets. Magpie, woodpecker, golden oriole, warbler, rooster, grouse, and nightingale, they are all disappearing, and the decline seems to be utterly beyond remedy.

Today we see ever-increasing hordes huddled together in our big cities, where they grow accustomed to the soot belching from the chimneys and the thunderous turmoil of the streets, where the nights are as bright as the days. These urban masses believe that they have had an adequate introduction to the world of nature as soon as they have caught a glimpse of a potato-field, or seen a single starling perched upon a branch of an emaciated road-side tree. But, to anyone who recalls the sounds and scents of the German landscape of seventy years ago, from out of the words and images in which these memories are embodied, a wind would arise to pronounce a warning reproach to the lost souls of today as soon as they begin to regurgitate their weather-proof platitudes about "economic development," "necessities," and "culture."

We express no opinion as to whence mere *utility* derives its deplorable authority over all modern transactions. Nor will we waste our time in belaboring a point that will soon become common knowledge; we merely state the simple fact that in no conceivable case will human beings ever meet with success in their attempt to "correct" nature. Wherever the population of song-birds dwindles, we find an immeasurable proliferation of blood-sucking insects and caterpillars, which can devour whole vineyards and forests in a matter of days; wherever one shoots the buzzard and exterminates the adder, a plague of mice swiftly erupts to bring destruction to the bee-hives. As a result, the fertilization of the clover, which depends upon the bees, will not occur. With the aid of improved weapons, hunters massacre the finest specimens of wild deer, thus bringing about the degeneration of the herd through the excess reproduction of the unfit survivors, in an environment without natural predators; and this unthinking slaughter will continue in this fashion until a serious reaction on the part of wounded nature springs up in exotic lands, in the shape of terrible epidemics, which fasten themselves to the heel of "civilized" Europe. This enables us to understand that the Far Eastern plague was, in actuality, the result of the wholesale marketing in Asia of the pelts of rodents such as the woodchuck. Let us put these facts aside in order that we may focus a bright ray of light upon the one, decisive point: these examples conclusively prove that the profits that are produced by these commercial transactions do not have the slightest connection with any pressing material needs.

What the Germans refer to as an "Alpine forest," is just a recently reforested stand; a true Alpine forest, as it appears to us in myth and saga, will spread itself all the way to the ends of the Earth. America, which during the time of the Indians was endowed with the richest forests on Earth, has now begun to import lumber; the few regions that export their timber, such as Hungary, Russia, Scandinavia, and Canada, will soon be the only regions endowed with a surplus. The "progressive" nations, taken as a whole, annually cut down three hundred and fifty thousand tons of timber for the production of paper, thereby cutting down one book every two minutes, and one magazine every second; we can appreciate, from these rough estimates alone, just how massive the production of these items in the "civilized" world really is. Someone should at least attempt to explain to us why it is necessary to inundate the world with such quantities of newspapers, scandal magazines, and fictional thrillers; should no explanation be forthcoming, we must consequently consider the cutting down of primeval forests to be an even greater offense.

The Italians annually hunt down millions of migratory birds along their coasts, and they perform this operation in the most gruesome manner; what they themselves do not consume, is packed up for export to England and France. Numbers will express this more clearly: in one example from 1909, a single vessel transported two hundred and sixty thousand living quails, who were shipped in narrow cages to England, where the poor creatures were kept in miserable conditions, until the quail fanciers got around to butchering them. On the Sorrento peninsula, year after year, the birds have been captured alive, in numbers ranging as high as five hundred thousand. For Egypt, the tally of the exterminated reaches three million, not counting the untold numbers of larks, ortolans, warblers, swallows, and nightingales who also perished. It was not hunger that required the slaughter of these plumed singers: they fell to luxury and greed. More gruesome still is the devastation directly attributable to the fashion industry, as we learn when we read about those greedy designers and merchants whose faculty of invention seems to have been inspired by Satan himself. In the words of the *Cri de Paris*: "The Parisian hatmakers annually utilize up to forty thousand swallows and sea-gulls. A London merchant purchased during the preceding year thirty-two thousand colibris, eighty thousand sea birds, and eight hundred thousand birds of different species. It is known that every year no fewer than three hundred million birds are killed to adorn our ladies of fashion. There are lands where distinctive species once gave a unique appearance to regions from which they have now vanished. To guarantee that the feathers and down retain their brilliance, they must be plucked from the bodies of the birds while they still live. That is why one may not hunt the poor creatures with guns, but with *nets*. These inhuman hunters tear the feathers from their victims, who must endure the sufferings of the great martyrs before they perish in horrendous convulsions."

Thinking of himself as well-bred, man refuses to acknowledge the existence of such awkward happenings, while his women callously adorn themselves with the melancholy trophies of the hunt. It need not be emphasized that every one of the animal species that we have listed, along with many others such as the "bird of paradise," are nearing extinction. Sooner or later, the same fate will befall every animal species, except for those whom man has destined for breeding or domestication.

The billions of animal pelts of North America, the countless blue foxes, sables, and Siberian ermines, all point to the excesses of the fashion industry. In Copenhagen, in the years since 1908, a corporation has been developing a "method of hunting whales in a more peaceful manner, and according to a new method," i.e., employing ocean-based factories, which process the carcasses immediately after the hunt. These "swimming" factories, during the course of the two following years, processed approximately five hundred thousand of the largest mammals on the Earth, and the day is swiftly approaching when the whale known to history will have become a mere museum exhibit.

For millennia the American buffalo, the prized game of the Indians, roamed the prairie. But scarcely had the European set foot on the continent, when a lawless and savage slaughter broke out, so that today the buffalo is over and done with. In time, the same sad spectacle will be enacted in Africa. In order to furnish our so-called civilized man with billiard balls, buttons, combs, and similar articles of great importance, the most recent calculations provided by Tournier of Paris indicate that eight hundred thousand kilograms of pure ivory are processed annually. The result is the yearly slaughter of fifty thousand of the most stupendous of the world's creatures. In the same way occurred the merciless killing of the antelope, the rhino, the wild horse, the kangaroo, the giraffe, the ostrich, and the gnu in the tropics, along with the polar bear, musk ox, arctic fox, walrus, and seal in the arctic zone. An unparalleled orgy of destruction has seized mankind, and it is "civilization" that has unleashed this lust for murder, so that the Earth withers before its noxious breath. These are indeed the fruits of "progress"!

All of these facts are well known. Well-meaning and warm-hearted individuals have raised the warning cry again and again during the past ten years, urging mankind to protect nature and to preserve regional traditions from abuse; unfortunately, neither the deepest causes for, nor the massive consequences of, the menace to nature have been comprehended. However, before we probe more deeply into these matters, we must continue to pronounce our accusation.

We need not concern ourselves with determining whether or not life extends beyond our world, or whether the Earth is, in fact, a living being (which was the belief of the ancients), or merely an unfeeling lump of "dead matter" (the modern view); it is only because the Earth endures, that the tracts of land, the play of clouds, the bodies of water, the cloak of plant life, and the ceaseless activity of the animal kingdom, have all been woven together in a profoundly animated totality, which gathers the individual creatures together as if within an ark, which, in turn, is itself closely bound together with the great events of the infinite universe. An indispensable harmony resounds in the clamorous storms of the planet, in the sublime bleakness of the wilderness, in the solemnity of the highest mountains, in the appealing melancholy of the endless heath, in the mysterious fabric of towering forests, and in the pulsating lightning of the sea-storm as it hurls its bolts against the coastline. Or this harmony may exist in a dreamy immersion in the primordial works of man. If, in a moment of profound reverie, we should direct our gaze upon the pyramids, the Sphinx, and the lotus-shaped capitals of Egypt's columns; or upon the brightly decorated bell-towers of the Chinese and the structural clarity of the Hellenic temple; or upon the warm domesticity of the Dutch farmhouse and the Tartar encampment on the open steppes: we perceive that all of these creations breathe the very soul of the landscape upon which they stand. Earlier cultures said that such structures had "sprung from the Earth"; thus, we too see that there is form and color in everything that has sprung from the Earth, from the dwellings to the weapons and household implements, the daggers, spears, axes, swords, necklaces, brooches, and rings, the elegant decorated vessels, the cakes filled with nuts, the vessels of copper, and the thousand-fold textures and fabrics. More frightful still than those items that we have already surveyed—albeit not quite so irremediable—are the effects of "progress" in the colonial regions. The connection between the works of man and the Earth has now been disrupted, shattering for centuries—perhaps permanently—the primordial song of the landscape.

Now railroad tracks, telegraph poles, and high-voltage power cables cut through the contours of forest and mountain; this can be seen not only in Europe, but in India, Egypt, Australia, and America as well. The gray, multi-level apartment blocks that stand attached to an endless row of identical structures, sprout up wherever an educated person wishes to display his ability to increase "prosperity." Everywhere, the rural fields are "combined" into rectangular plots, ancient grave-sites are disturbed, thriving nurseries are obliterated, the reed-bordered fishponds dry up, and the flourishing forested wilderness of yesteryear has had to surrender its pristine state, because all trees must now line up like soldiers, and every woodland must be purged of the old thickets of "poisonous" undergrowth; the winding rivers which once suspended themselves in glittering, labyrinthine curves, must now become perfectly straight canals; the swift streams and waterfalls—and this is true even for Niagara—must now feed electric power plants; ever-expanding forests of smokestacks reach all the way to the oceans' shores; and the water pollution caused by industry transforms nature's pristine waters into raw sewage. Very soon, the face of the Earth will be transformed into a gigantic Chicago, pocked with a few patches of agriculture! "My God," cried out the noble Achim von Arnim at the beginning of the last century, "where are the old trees, under which we still rode only yesterday? And what has happened to the ancient inscriptions carved upon the boundary stones? These things are already forgotten by our people, and nothing could be sadder than to see us striking against our own roots. When the peak of a towering mountain has been but once stripped of its timber, no timber will ever grow there again; my mission is to see that Germany's heritage will not be squandered!" And Lenau's impressions of the landscape of our homeland made him feel that nature has been stuffed up to the throat so that blood spurts from her every pore. What would these men have to say to us today! Perhaps they might, like Heinrich von Kleist, decide to quit the Earth, whose son, man himself, has brought such shame upon his head. "The devastation of the Thirty Years' War did not bring about such fundamental alterations of the heritage of the past in town and countryside as the obsession of modern life with its ruthless, one-sided pursuit of practical purposes." (From the announcement of the establishment of the "League for Nature Preservation.") However, as regards the hypocritical "nature feeling" of the tourist trade, we need hardly direct our attention to the devastation which its "exploitation" of remote coastal regions and mountain valleys leaves in its wake. Even these matters were comprehensively addressed, again and yet again, but the effort was wasted. The complete presentation was developed by 1880 through the efforts of the first-rate writer Rudorff, to whose 1910 essay "On the Relation of Modern Life to Nature" we would direct every reader's attention.

As if those things were not enough, the rage for extermination has now dragged its bloody furrow through mankind himself. Tribal populations have dwindled, and some tribes have even vanished. Some were exterminated or starved to death, while others succumbed to disease; all were forced to accept the blessings of "progress": brandy, opium, and syphilis. The Indians are over and done with; the Australian aborigines are finished; the noblest Polynesians are at their last gasp; the most courageous African warriors have fought the good fight, but now they too must give way to "civilization"; and Europe has just seen an equally courageous folk, Europe's last primordial tribe, the Albanians — those "Eagle-sons," whose ancestry can be traced directly back to the legendary "Pelasgians" — methodically killed, by the thousands, at the hands of the Serbs.

Make no mistake: "progress" is the lust for power and nothing besides, and we must unmask its method as a sick, destructive joke. Utilizing such pretexts as "necessity," "economic development," and "culture," the final goal of "progress" is nothing less than the destruction of life. This destructive urge takes many forms: progress is devastating forests, exterminating animal species, extinguishing native cultures, masking and distorting the pristine landscape with the varnish of industrialism, and debasing the organic life that still survives. It is the same for livestock as for the mere commodity, and the boundless lust for plunder will not rest until the last bird falls. To achieve this end, the whole weight of technology has been pressed into service, and at last we realize that technology has become by far the largest domain of the sciences.

Let us pause here for a moment. In a certain sense, even man belongs to nature; some even suggest that man belongs entirely to nature; as we will see, that is certainly an erroneous view. In any case, when something within him struggles with life, it is not, after all, struggling with man himself. Our chain of evidence will lose its most important links if we do not also offer illustrations of the self-demoralization of mankind.

The roll call of the dead, which could be inscribed here, even were it to be restricted to the most important names, would far exceed the list of fallen animals. It will suffice to commemorate a few prominent victims:

where are the popular festivals and sacred customs, which for uncounted millennia served as perpetual springs for myth and poetry? Where is now the rider on the meadow who sows the precious seeds? And where can we find the procession of the Pentecostal bride and the torch-bearer running through the cornfields? Where is now the intricate richness of traditional costume, in which every folk could express its own nature, on its own landscape? The rich pendants, the multicolored bodices, the decorated waistcoats, sashes adorned with precious metals, and the light sandals? Where can we find now the toga-styled shawls, the pleated turbans, and flowing kimonos? They are all being replaced by "civilized" attire. Throughout the world civilization distributes the three-piece suit for the men, and for the women — the latest Parisian style.

Where now do we find the folk-song, that ever-renewed treasury of melody, which cloaks with its fabric of silver man's advancing age and passing away. Wedding-feast and solemn wake, revenge, war, and destruction, drunkenness and wanderlust, the feeling of a child and the delight of a mother, all of these things breathe and stream in inexhaustible songs, which can swiftly provoke one to a fiery action, or swiftly cradle another in the sleep of forgetfulness. There were once poems and songs composed for the dance, for the brimming goblet, for farewell and homecoming, for consecration and magical incantation, for the dusk that falls in the spinning room; before the battle, and at the bier of the slain, one was stirred by songs of scorn, by martial anthems of a dark-bright poetry blending mountain, spring, and shrub, the animals of the household, wild game and plant, the force of the wind and the torrent of rain. Even work was felt to be a kind of festival, a feeling that has long since been inconceivable to us. Song was not reserved solely for roving and revelry; song accompanied the hoisting of the anchor, the rhythm of the oar-stroke, the shifting of heavy cargo, the towing of the ship, the stowing of the casks, the blacksmith's hammering, and the rowing of the oarsmen; there was song for the mowing, threshing, and grinding of the corn, and for the picking, braiding, and weaving of the flax. Not only has "progress" made life gray, it has also silenced life's very voice. But no — we forget that after the primordial melody of the popular ballads comes the operetta and the syrupy idioms of the cabaret; after legendary musical instruments like the Spanish guitar, the Italian mandolin, the Finnish kantela, the gusli of the Southern Slavs, and the Russian balalaika, there comes the piano and the record player. There we have the fruits of "progress"! Like an all-devouring conflagration, "progress" scours the Earth, and the place that has fallen to its flames, will flourish nevermore, so long as man still survives. The animal- and plant-species cannot renew themselves, man's innate warmth of heart has gone, the inner springs that once nurtured the flourishing songs and sacred festivals are blocked, and there remains only a wretched and cold working day and the hollow show of noisy "entertainment." There can be no doubt: we are living in the era of the downfall of the soul.

There would still be large personalities under such circumstances! We certainly do not wish to underestimate the ingenuity of the masters of technology, nor the computational talent of our captains of industry. Nevertheless, if one placed such mere talent alongside a true creator's strength, we must surely come to the conclusion that technology is without the slightest capacity to enrich life. The cleverest machine has meaning only in the service of a purpose, and even the most extensive industrial organization of today will be nothing in a thousand years; whereas the poetry of Homer, the wise words of Heraclitus, and the symphonies of Beethoven belong to the undying treasures of life. But how sad we become, when we think of those who once were justly proclaimed to us as the most illustrious of men, when we look at our poets and thinkers of today! Whom do we still have, since the veterans of the spirit and the deed have departed: Burckhardt, Böcklin, Bachofen, Mommsen, Bismarck, Keller, and even Nietzsche, the last flame from that old fire, all of them gone without a trace, without a successor! It is as empty up on Parnassus, as it is in politics and thought, and we will maintain a discreet silence regarding the putrefying arts. When we come down to the level of everyday life, we can see very clearly the total nihilism behind all the commonplace chatter about "personality" and "culture."

Most men do not really live, they merely exist: some to be used up as if they were mere machines in the service of some great undertaking, and some to be reduced to the status of money's slaves, deliriously busying themselves with the value of stocks and bonds; some, finally, attach themselves to the frenzied diversions offered by the big city. Many, likewise, are oppressed by the wretched and ever-increasing tedium of this existence. In no earlier time was unhappiness greater or more poisonous. Groups of men, large or small, whose members are bound each to the other in the furtherance of some special interest, struggle endlessly to destroy their enemies. Such enmity may arise from commercial, political, racial, or religious grounds. At times one may discover such crazed power-struggles even within a single association. Humans the world over always seem to project their own prejudices onto their environment. Thus, man foists his own obsession with status and power onto nature, wherein he swiftly discovers a wild struggle for existence; he convinces himself that he must have been in the right if he alone survived this struggle for existence; and he paints the world in the guise of a great machine, where the pistons only give off the steam that must turn the wheels, in order that "energy"—one does not see to what end—will be transferred, and he accompanies all of this with a bit of idle chatter about the so-called "philosophy of monism," which utterly falsifies the billion-fold life of nature in order to reduce the universe to the level of the human ego. Where one previously prized love, or renunciation, or a god-intoxicated withdrawal from the world, we find instead a newly hatched success-religion, which is announced, from atop the graves of former ages, to those of little faith, whose coming had been anticipated by Nietzsche, who, with white-hot scorn and a knowing wink, makes his "last man" proclaim: "We have invented happiness!"

Of course, the superficial errors in all of these systems, sects, and tendencies will not be with us for very much longer. Nature knows no "struggle for existence," but only a *caring for life*. Many insects die after the act of procreation, thus demonstrating the slight emphasis that nature places upon mere preservation. Nature only ensures that similar forms will continue to unfold amid the surging waves of life. What prompts one animal to hunt another to the death is simply the need to appease the predator's hunger; greed, ambition, and the lust for power have no place here. In reality, there is a gaping abyss here that no evolutionary logic will ever bridge. Species were never exterminated by other species, since every excess on one side is followed almost immediately by a reciprocal reaction on the other; the ranks of the vanquished are thinned, and the booty of the slain foe becomes the sustenance of the stronger. Transformation, however, is consummated over gigantic periods of time, and invariably leads to a burgeoning of lower life-forms in the vicinity. The annihilation of hundreds of species during the course of mankind's earthly tenure permits no point of comparison with the wholesale extinction of the dinosaur and the mammoth.

Utterly mindless, moreover, is the transfer of the numerically quantifiable operations of the physical laws that govern the conservation of energy, to questions of *life*. No single living cell has ever been created in a chemical retort, and should science ever announce such an achievement, it will not have been as a result of some combination of physical forces, but because even the chemical matter with which such an experiment must begin is already imbued with the instinct for life. Life is an enduring, perpetual renewal of formative power; and we extinguish some measure of such power whenever we exterminate a living species, and the Earth will be impoverished till the end of time because of it, regardless of any detriment to the so-called law of *conservation of energy.*

As we have said, such erroneous teachings will fade and perish eventually, but the resulting, all-too-real eventualities that they have brought to pass will remain, making all those conceptual schemes seem more like mere shadows of thought than the genuine article. There is certainly no basis for the opinion that considers the ongoing destruction to be a mere side-effect of passing conditions, out of which will arise some sort of attempt at reconstruction. With that we arrive at the meaning of the preceding course of events to which man has given the name "world history."

The ancient Greeks had no skill with electrical wiring, power cables, and radios, and this fact sheds light on their habitual scorn for physical science, which they saw as a rather lowly business. But only they could construct temples, carve images on columns, and cut precious gems, of such beauty and delicacy, that we can only compete with them by making use of our most artificial tools! Without conducting experiments, and supported only by everyday perception, the Greek philosophers have influenced, and in large part governed, the course of Western thought for over two millennia. The didactic virtue of Socrates has been revived in the scrawnier "categorical imperative" of Kant; the Platonic "doctrine of the Ideas" has been revived in the aesthetics of Schopenhauer; and the philosophical framework of the atomistic theory of chemistry stems directly from Democritus. Faced with these facts, is it not more likely that the Greeks avoided physical science not because of their lack of capacity for such study, but because they chose not to have any dealings with it? Perhaps their mystics might enable us to recover many insights that have been lost to us? Let us take another example: the Chinese of Antiquity would have seen all our modern discoveries as alien to their culture; the modern Chinese would feel the same way towards these discoveries, had we not compelled China to accept them by force. We are likewise impressed by the great Chinese philosophers, sages such as Lao Tse or Lei Zi, who speak to us in words of such wisdom that even Goethe seems a mere bungler by comparison. Thus, if the Chinese did not possess a science with whose assistance they might have been able to build cannons,

(The Spirit as Adversary of the Soul) must, in addition, feel a certain amazement at Meingast's ravings concerning the necessity for a "determined will"! Another familiar (and depressing) insight into the resistance mounted by even sympathetic writers to the biocentric philosophy can be derived from a perusal of Musil's *Tagebücher* (Diaries), with its dreary and philistine insistence that the Klagesian rapture must at all costs be constrained by *Geist*, by its pallid praise for a "daylight mysticism," and so on. Admittedly, *Der Mann ohne Eigenschaften* will remain an astonishing and beautifully-crafted masterpiece of twentieth century *belles lettres*, in spite of its author's jejune "philosophical" preachments.

During this same period, Klages rediscovered the late-Romantic philosopher Carl Gustav Carus, author of the pioneering *Psyche: Zur Entwicklungsgeschichte der Seele* (Psyche: Towards a Developmental History of the Soul) in which the unconscious is moved to center-stage (sadly, the Jung-racket falsely credits their master with this discovery). The very first sentence of this work indicates the primacy attributed by Carus to the unconscious: "The key to the understanding of the conscious life of the soul lies in the realm of the unconscious." During the Romantic revival that took place in the Germany of the 1920s, Klages would edit a new, abridged version of *Psyche*, in which Carus is purged of his logocentric and Christian errors. Klages, however, fully accepts Carus' definition of the soul as synonymous with life, a formulation that he rates as epochally significant. He finds Carus' statement to be as profound as the aphorism of Novalis in which he locates the soul at the point of contact between the inner and outer worlds.

In 1913, Klages presented his *Zur Theorie und Symptomatologie des Willens* (On the Theory and Symptomatology of the Will) to the Vienna Congress of International Societies for Medical Psychology and Psychotherapy. In that same year, Klages delivered an address entitled "Mensch und Erde" to a gathering of members of the German Youth Movement. This seminal work has recently received its due as the "foundational" document of the "deep ecology" movement when a new edition was published in 1980 in coordination with the establishment of the German "Green" political party.

In his *Heidnische Feuerzeichen* (Pagan Fire-Signs), which was completed in 1913, although it would not be published in book form until 1944, Klages has some very perceptive remarks on consciousness, which he regards as always effect and never cause. He cautions us to realize that, because our feelings are almost always conscious, we tend to attribute far blow up mountains, and grace their tables with margarine, it is because they had no desire for these things. Behind the scenes, certain forces are controlling mankind, and it is only by examining these forces that we can understand a crucial fact: before the progressive research of modern times could be undertaken, the intellectuals had to be conditioned to adopt a philosophical theory upon which would be founded a required practice: we call that practice capitalism.

No intelligent person can have the slightest doubt that the dazzling achievements of physics and chemistry have been pressed into the exclusive service of "capital." The identifying characteristic of modern science is its substitution of numerical quantities for unique qualities, thus merely recapitulating, in the cognitive form, the fundamental law that the will must control everything, even that which resides in the brightly-colored domain of the soul and its values: the values of blood, beauty, dignity, ardor, grace, warmth, and the maternal sense; these must yield to the insidious values of the power which judges the *worth* of a man by the weight of his gold. A new word for this viewpoint has even been coined: "Mammonism." Nevertheless, how few are conscious of the fact that this "Mammon" is a genuine, substantial entity, which seizes hold of man, and wields him as if he were a mere tool that might help Mammon eradicate the life of the Earth. Let us provide here a brief word of explanation.

We have already indicated that "progress," "civilization," and "capitalism" constitute different manifestations of the same direction of the will. We must likewise admit that the disciples of this will-centered worldview are drawn exclusively from the Christian world. Only within that world were the inventions accumulated; only within that world was that quantifying, "exact" scientific methodology brought to perfection; and, finally, only within that world, that Christian world which is perpetually engaged in the most ruthless imperialism imaginable, could one find those men who have sought to conquer all of the non-Christian races, just as they have sought to conquer the whole of nature. Consequently, we are compelled to locate the proximate causes of world-historical "progress" in Christianity itself. On the surface, of course, Christianity seems always to be preaching sermons in praise of "love," but when we take a closer look at this "love," we discover that in reality this persuasive word functions as a gilded surface which masks the underlying reality of a categorical *command*: "you must"; and this unconditional command applies solely to man, who has now come to consider himself as divine, as a god standing in opposition to the whole of nature. Christianity may mouth such phrases as "the welfare of mankind," or "humanity," but what the voice inside these formulas is really saying is that no other living being has the slightest intrinsic value or purpose, except in so far as it can be forced to serve the purposes of *man*. From time immemorial, the "love" of the Christian has never prevented him from persecuting religious pagans with a murderous hatred; and this same "love" does not prevent him even now from abolishing the sacred rituals of conquered tribal cultures. It is a well-known fact that Buddhism proscribes the killing of animals, because the Buddhist recognizes the obvious fact that each and every earthly creature shares a common nature with man himself. But when one objects to the Italian's murdering of an animal, he will immediately respond by assuring you that the creature "has no soul," and "is not a Christian." This indicates clearly that, for the devout Christian, only man has a right to live. To the people of the ancient world, religion, which at one time also proceeded according to this pattern that even now springs up in hovels of the people, restrains its standard bearer, and yet it excites him on the other hand, and permits the power of one who threatens the peace of the world to prosper until it has become the terrifying megalomania that considers the bloodiest offenses against life to be permitted, and even *commanded*, provided such deeds result in "benefits" to humanity. Capitalism, along with its pathfinder, science, is in point of fact the *fulfillment* of Christianity; the church, like science, constitutes a consortium of special interests; and the "one" that is addressed by a secularized morality is indistinguishable from the life-hostile "ego," which, in the name of the unique godhead of the spirit — only now coupled with a blind cosmology — accounts for the war that has been waged against the innumerable, "many" gods of the world; earlier ages were at least more *honest* in their opposition to the cosmic deities, for they frankly approached the fray in the menacing aspect of *judges*.

> Icy northern winds have gone
> To devastate the blooms of May;
> To make us worship only ONE,
> A world of gods must fade away!

— Friedrich Schiller, *"The Gods of Greece"*

By now it should be perfectly clear, however, that he who seeks to enrich himself—whilst he stomps Earth's blossoms into dust—is man as the bearer of calculating reason and the will-to-acquisition. The gods whom he has torn from the tree of life are the perpetually changing images of the phenomenal world, from which he has exiled himself. The hostility to images, which was inwardly nurtured by the self-lacerating Middle Ages, had to emerge into the light of day, as soon as it had achieved its goal, which was to sever the bond connecting man to the soul of the Earth. In man's bloody atrocities against his fellow creatures, he could only complete that which he himself had already begun: to exchange the multiform patterns of living images for the homeless transcendence of the world-alienated spirit. He has shown enmity to the planet that bore and nursed him, and even to the revolutions of the starry heavens, because he is now possessed by a power that resembles a *vampire*, which introduces into the "music of the spheres" sounds of an ear-shattering dissonance. At this point it is clear, however, that in the course of this very ancient evolutionary process, Christianity signifies but one epoch; from distant beginnings, this process has now reached its final stage. Certainly, the unique physiognomy of Europe was decisively shaped by this process.

In fact, the force that provokes man's enmity against the world is precisely as old as "world history"! The "history" that is surnamed the *evolutionary process*—which in the course of events marches beyond, and ever onwards, and cannot be compared to the *destiny* of other organisms—begins at the very moment of man's expulsion from "paradise," when he finds himself on the outside, seeing now with the cold, clear gaze of the stranger, and knowing that he has lost his previous accord with plants and animals, with oceans and clouds, with rocks, winds, and stars. In the myths of almost every people we encounter bloody battles in pre-historic ages between solar heroes who are bent upon installing a new order and the "chthonic" powers of fate, who are finally banished into a lightless underworld. Nevertheless, a Jesuit scholar, in an astonishing, but instructive, reversal of circumstances, has discovered in the legend of the acts of the Greek Heracles a prophetic "plagiarism" of the life of the Christian redeemer! That above-mentioned reorganization, with which history begins, is always and everywhere the same: over the soul rises the spirit, over the dream reigns a wide-awake rationality, over life, which becomes and passes, there stands purposeful activity. During the millennial development of spirit, Christianity was only the final, crucial thrust. Therefore spirit, which emerged from a condition of powerless knowledge—Prometheus is in chains, while Heracles is free!—now penetrates the will, and in murderous deeds, which have constituted, without interruption, the history of nations ever since, has revealed a truth that had heretofore seemed to be merely a notion: that a power from outside our cosmos had broken into the sphere of life.

For that reason, our dearest desire is simply for everyone to open his eyes. Further, we should desist from all attempts to blend together things that are sundered by the profound abyss that separates the powers of love and the soul on one side, from the powers of reason and will on the other. We must perceive that the very essence of the will is manifest in its compulsion to tear the "veil of *maya*" to tatters; for when man has been reduced to the status of a mere creature of will, he must, in a blind rage, set his hand against his own mother, the Earth. In the end, all of life, along with man himself, will be swallowed up by nothingness.

No teaching can return us to that which has once been lost. Regarding all such attempts, we feel that man simply does not have the ability to bring about a transformation of his inner life on his own. We stated earlier that the ancients never presumed to unravel nature's secrets by means of experiments, and never thought to conquer her through the use of machines, which they dismissed as clever contraptions that were suitable only for slaves; we now insist, moreover, that they abhorred such attempts as *ungodliness*. Forest and spring, boulder and grotto were for them filled with sacred life; from the summits of their lofty mountains blew the stormwinds of the gods (it was not from lack of a "feeling for nature" that one did not climb their peaks!), and tempest and hailstones threatened or clashed furiously in the play of battle. When the Greeks desired to construct a bridge across a stream, they begged the river deity to pardon this deed of man for which they atoned by offering up to him a sacrificial libation of wine. In ancient German lands, an offense against a living tree was expiated by the shedding of the offender's blood. Today's mankind sees only childish superstition in those who attend to the planetary currents. He forgets that the interpreting of apparitions was a way of scattering blooms around the tree of an inner life, which shelters a deeper knowledge than all of science: *the knowledge of the world-weaving power of all-embracing love.* Only when this love has been renewed in mankind will the wounds inflicted by the matricidal spirit be healed.

It was a mere hundred years ago that something truly new welled up within the hearts of men, as if from out of the depths of mysterious springs: we are alluding to those unforgettable dreamers, those child-like sages and poets, whom we conventionally call the "Romantics." Their expectations were illusory and their storm has subsided; their wisdom has been buried, the flood has receded, and the "desert grows." Nevertheless, we are prepared, like the Romantics, to believe in miracles, and we are quite willing to deem it possible that a coming generation may indeed see the birth of a new world. Perhaps the visionary words of Eichendorff in "Foreboding and the Present" best describe the labor pains that must precede the birth of that world:

Our age seems to me to resemble an ever-expanding, uncertain twilight. Light and shadow battle still, powerful forces that appear to be inseparable; storm-clouds brew dark destinies, and no one can tell whether their portents indicate death or benediction; and the wider world below remains abandoned to its hollow expectations. Comets and celestial messages haunt the heavens once more, phantom spirits wander through the night, and mythical sirens plummet into the sea as if they fled in dread of some approaching tempest that has already obscured the mirror-surface of the waters; they sing, gesticulating with bloody fingers, warning us of some terrible, impending doom. No carefree childhood game or frolic can delight our young people as much as those sessions of long ago, during which our forefathers prepared us for the serious side of life. We are born in battle, and, regardless of whether we are victor or vanquished, we will perish in battle. For, from out of the magical mists of our schooldays, there takes shape the Ghost of War, clad in armor, with the pallid face of death, and with blood-spattered hair; his eyes are well-accustomed to solitude, and they already perceive, through the webs of smoke that swirl all around, the almost imperceptible outlines of the coming struggle. Woe to those who, when the hour of battle strikes, find themselves unarmed and utterly unprepared for combat! How many weak men, who fritter away their idle hours in the pursuit of pleasure and in frivolous reflections, who manage to deceive themselves as readily as they deceive the world, will recall the words of Prince Hamlet: 'The time is out of joint; O cursed spite/That ever I was born to set it right!' Then, out of the collapse of the world, will emerge once more an unprecedented contest between the old and the new, and the passions of today that slink about in disguise, will find that their masks are now disparaged. A burning frenzy will burst with flaming torch held high into the pandemonium, as if the inferno itself had been loosed upon the world. Justice and injustice will seem to have merged their natures in a blind access of rage. But miracles will at last take place, and the just will receive their just rewards; and a new, yet somehow very ancient, sun will radiate its light through the scenes of horror. The thunder will still roll, but only upon the peaks of distant mountains; and then the white dove will soar aloft in the clear blue skies; and the Earth itself will shine with a brighter light from the heavens above.

On Ethics (1918)

W hat does our moralist really want? Obviously, he wants to "improve" man ethically, and to keep on improving him, until, finally, perfection graces the Earth. Of course, there can be no doubt as to the moralist's good intentions and no one would wish to cast aspersions on the "purity" of his heart. But it is also obvious from the outset that he has not the slightest inclination to open up for critical discussion such issues as how he intends to accomplish his purpose and how he has achieved such certainty as to the correctness of that purpose. Nor does he seem at all eager to disclose just who or what has charged him with his mission to change everything that lives and breathes. We might also wish to enquire of him whether or not his program of "improvement" has the slightest prospect of success!

Ethical codes are always presented to us by their apologists as if they were solid structures standing firmly upon the bedrock of facts. Nevertheless, the moralist, who regards man and the world as interchangeable terms, is not permitted to draw any conclusions from an examination of the behavior of "man" as he conducts himself in the visions of poets and dreamers. The moralist must instead focus his attention solely upon the mankind whose exploits constitute the chronicle known as "world history." On this matter, we can quite easily demonstrate something that everyone should surely comprehend even without our assistance: that the mankind of blood, murder, betrayal, violence, and greed, is without even a superficial resemblance to the product of wishful thinking that inhabits the brain of the moralist. It is the intention of the moralist that everyone around him should "improve" himself. He transports his "idea of the good" into the future, which he always finds to be a more congenial place than the sorry present: previously, mankind was malicious and vile, and even now, admittedly, he possesses these vicious traits in abundance. But hearken! Man will now improve himself more and more until, perhaps, some fine day in the distant future, he will draw nigh to the realization of the "idea of the good," albeit there is only a slim chance that he will, in point of fact, attain to the highest pitch of perfection. The moralist is alone in his conviction that the fulfillment of his expectations really lies within the realm of possibility. But how will he go about changing the crimes and the misdeeds that have already occurred? How could history's countless millions of villains—known and unknown—the backbiters, the poisoners of hearts, the jealous, the dishonorable, the slanderers, the schemers, and the parasites (both physical and spiritual), be improved so long after we have buried their corpses? Or does our moralist restrict membership in his "mankind" to those now living? Or is he talking about those particularly fortunate men who have been cunning enough to postpone the hour of their birth to a later century when, at long last, these illustrious ethical ideals shall have been brought to fruition? Will a single atrocity that transpired in an earlier time be negated, or minimized, merely because some future generation—I know not which—will finally rejoice in having attained to complete moral perfection? How little truth there is in the moralist's schemes will, perhaps, be made somewhat clearer if we ponder, for a moment, the fortunes of those doomed souls who were forced to suffer under the vile French Revolutionary government, with its treason, deceit, lawlessness, theft, betrayal, and every conceivable form of torture!

Let us consider the bitter anger of nobles who, with gnashing of teeth, humiliated themselves by groveling before their vicious revolutionary captors, lest a proud demeanor offend their jailers and lead to their heads being hacked off; the pain and anguish of the myriad victims who fell to the bloodsucking guillotine; and the helpless endurance of shame and betrayal by the guiltless. Are they, somehow, to have their sufferings cancelled or ameliorated retroactively, as it were, because, after the lapse of some unspecified number of millennia, a spotless generation shall have inherited the Earth? Just as it is certain that an event that has transpired can never be transformed into a "non-event," it is equally certain that no rational person can conceive of "improving" those who have already been buried in an "unimproved" state! I might draw your attention here to the affinity that exists between these ridiculous schemes for moral improvement and two of the fundamental doctrines of Christianity. The first is the curious notion that mere "faith" in the mission of the Christian redeemer "makes blessed." However one interprets this doctrine, such

blessedness can only benefit a limited segment of mankind, for it per-
tains only to those individuals who were born after a certain point in
history. As a matter of fact, there were not a few simpletons during the
late Middle Ages who were absolutely certain that Plato and Aristotle,
even if they had managed to avoid hellfire, were at least suffering the
torments of purgatory! The second Christian doctrine holds that the first
priority on "Doomsday" will be answering the divine accountant's questions regarding *profit* and *loss*; there is no need for us to make any further
comment on that piece of information!

In aiming at this pretended improvement of mankind, nothing — and
whoever denies this is something of a deceiver — *nothing* takes precedence before natural good faith, in other words, a faith that is guileless, unconscious, and, hence, *instinctual*. Deceit plants itself within the
heart; the head, as always, will manage to concoct reasons with which to
reinforce a predetermined faith.

The mere practitioner of ethics would not, of course, force the issue;
if mankind has hitherto shown no interest in being saved, the practical
moralist would merely comment that his true concern is with the living
and the yet unborn. On bended knee, he will pronounce his fervent
wish that such and such evil deeds shall never again come to pass. The
theoretician of ethics, however — the one who is, so to speak, "in the
know" — need make no concessions. Thus, because he has nothing to
say about the "eternal law" and the "absolute good" (although he himself certainly aspires to their realization), he will explain that the whole
project of "improvement" is nothing more than a hygienic measure, as if
one were to drain a swamp that is swarming with infectious mosquitoes
or send the shoe that is pinching one's foot to the shoemaker for repairs.
In order to achieve his goals, he employs no "moral claim," no "categorical imperative"; instead, he mouths those more or less emphatic phrases
with which one provides oneself in order to emphasize one's devotion to
duty. Let us now revert to the true moralist.

We have seen that the very idea of "improving" mankind is a pious
self-deception, because, regardless of how much improvement occurs in
mankind, in the long run, every human being must, alas, die and de-
compose. Now we ask ourselves if it is only the improvement of future
generations that is to enter into the moralist's reckoning. But are not
we ourselves — the living and the present — the bodily, psychical, and
spiritual descendants of the same mankind that oozed bloody murder
and vileness long before we came upon the scene? Does not their blood

course through our veins and arteries? We think of ourselves as being racially pure members of an advanced, "guileless" stock; but is it not the case that the future will infallibly bring about an ever-increasing process of racial bastardization? And does not such racial pollution infect only the innocent, and never those—we have no need to speak the name of the tribe aloud—who are the unrecognized criminals of the heart? Do we not find, throughout history, that the party of the degenerate always triumphs over the party of the noble? Is it really necessary that we trot out every scrap of irrefutable evidence that proves our point? Constantine the so-called "Great," Charles the so-called "Great" (Charlemagne), Gregory, Torquemada, Cortés, Cromwell, Robespierre, and so many others: is it not true that the only essential distinctions to be drawn between such characters concern the measure of horror and destructiveness with which each one conducts his orgies of mass murder? Yet it is these same so-called "great men"—whose actions have set mankind upon the road that he now travels, and whose careers have determined the destiny of succeeding generations—whom we insist upon calling the "great"! It is less the noble souls than the criminal spirits, in other words, those who have created, and still create today, the history of the world, who comprise our ancestral heritage. With a very great semblance of truth, one might say that we are engaged in the incessant *debasement* of mankind.

Meanwhile, the ethical teacher retorts, if at any time the ethical idea were to achieve complete success, or only partial success, or even no success whatsoever, that would have no bearing on the issue, for the "Ideal" would endure and would advance its inviolate demands, and only the demands of this "Ideal" deserve man's attention. The success or failure of his actions is not decisive for the moralist, and should his efforts run aground a hundred times in a row, the "good" would still remain, no less than before, the guiding principle of his striving. However, we might wish to examine these ideals of his a bit more closely at this juncture.

In earlier publications I adduced many reasons that lead us to the conclusion that we must examine the relationship between two ultimate and irreducible principles in order to account for the history of man; and I have further indicated that these two powers stand in opposition to each other, and that the degree to which one of these powers gains ascendancy entails the reciprocal weakening of the other. Regardless of the verbal form in which this insight makes its appearance, the truth behind the insight can and must be demonstrated. On the other hand, there is certainly no conclusive explanation as to why each individual must affiliate himself with one party or the other; perhaps it is merely a personal disposition which determines which of the parties to the dispute one holds to be a constructive force and which is seen as a destructive one. Let us elaborate: I call the one +x, so I must call the other –y; on the other hand, when I speak of –x, there must also be a correlative +y. The customary names for that which appears to me to be the constructive power and, thus, the +x, are nature, sensuality, and heart. More precise and correct terms would be life, cosmos, and soul. My –y, consequently, would be will, deed, *Logos*, mind, "idea," "God," "supreme being," the pure subject, the absolute ego, and spirit. At present, one side of the ledger is recognized by our ethical teachers, an admission that is attended by a qualification, for they feel that the concession of which we speak in no way entails agreement with any imputation of "dualism" to the constitution of man. They deny as well that the "idea of the good" stems from nature. Above all, however, they deny with all of the force that is in them our view that between the two opposed forces, spirit and soul, there exists a relationship of opposition or hostility. On the contrary, they assure us that nature is an "exposition" or "revelation" of the "idea of the good." Before we prove conclusively that they have already landed themselves in insuperable logical contradictions, we might examine the provenance of their opinions with some profit.

The "idea of the good" is characterized from the outset by the making of demands or, in other words, by the giving of commands. More than that, it is, so to speak, the "command in itself," the absolute command, the old categorical imperative! Thus, whoever maintains this point of view reveals that it is precisely in introducing this "categorical imperative" into the spatio-temporal world that he concedes that the world itself was brought into being by a command. But that claim differs not in the least from the Mosaic creation-myth; it is identical to the procedure employed by Yahweh, the God of the Jews. And let us avail ourselves of this opportunity to put our finger on the reason why this Mosaic idea, which has no parallel among other cultures, is without a doubt the most preposterous sort of impudence: such arrogant impostures could never have arisen among healthy natures. They have survived among us only because the inhabitants of Christendom have had these lunatic fables drummed into their heads since childhood; as a result, they can never escape from idiocies in comparison with which all of our extant ghost stories and fairy tales have the appearance of truth. One laughs at those who believe in ghosts, one mocks at the fetishes and idols of "primitive" tribes, one considers it to be an astounding phantom of the brain when the Orphic theologians of ancient Greece sought the origin of the world in the primeval ovum; one does not even notice that no cosmogony ever devised by the mind of man possesses a fraction of the absurdity inherent in the Mosaic world-creation on demand! For no command can ever have the power to create one single object, not even the rain-drop that beats upon my window-pane.

When the sergeant shouts the order "Halt!" or "March!", is the energy that sets the soldier in motion released as soon as the command is issued, or does it require the living force embodied in the soldier who hears it? What holds true in this case holds true in every other. Surely the command cannot produce results by itself, for it always requires the innate responsive force of the person who has heard it. In other words, the command requires the whole spatio-temporal world, particularly its vital energy and, ultimately, a conscious mind within that world, to recognize the existence of the command: without such responsive recognition, it is nothing.

The Mosaic creation myth, on the other hand, maintains that a mere command brought forth the entire universe out of nothingness. And the identical procedure holds for the ethical teacher when he explains the spatio-temporal actuality as a phenomenal reproduction of his "idea of the good," of the categorical imperative, of the absolute demand. Whereas, however, he somehow suppresses as an unholy fiction the opposition between the two powers of spirit and soul, a view that he can never endorse, he is forced back upon his own theory. Therefore, as we now wish to demonstrate, that which he preaches is, in fact, nothing but *mortal hostility to life*! We now understand that he is compelled to weave his phantoms in order to conceal this hostility from himself, for very few men of the modern age have the courage to admit that the battle between the two hostile powers even exists. Here, we must go all the way back to the so-called "Dark Ages," even back to the apologists and "Fathers of the Church," to encounter those—such as the agitator Augustine—whose basic viewpoint was that God's crucial commandment requires that we flee the "world of the senses." With those ancient ethical teachers one can come to an understanding of sorts. Each party can admit to the other that they represent two irreconcilably hostile powers, and thus they are in basic agreement on at least one crucial point. The opposition is crystal clear: they believe in the unyielding strife between Heaven and Hell. Each party, of course, sees Heaven in what the other regards to be Hell. On the other hand, no reconciliation is possible with the ethical teacher of today, who wages war against life, and who has no inclination to parley with the enemy. Like the Church Father, he stands on the side of the enemies of life, but, unlike them, he is ignorant, he hides behind a mask, he is a liar: *and he is devoid of self-understanding.* But let us now proceed to the conclusive proof of his self-contradiction!

What is the very essence of a command or an order? One must answer: a precept. But what exactly is a precept? To this we respond: always and everywhere it is a prohibition! The commands say, of course, "You must." In general, there is clearly no incentive in ordering someone to do that which he is quite prepared to do on his own. As we all know, however, he does *not* do whatever it is that we would command him to do "on his own," and so he must be prompted by a command. Without a doubt, his actions would be quite different in the absence of the command; a different command would likewise bring about a different outcome. Thus we must ask: wherein lies the essential nature of the moral command? And we must respond: in the suppression of a vital process or condition. I have scarcely opened the pages of the Roman Catholic catechism when I discover that, out of the "Ten Commandments," seven employ the formula "Thou shalt not," whilst the remaining three take the "Thou shalt" form. But it requires no great critical astuteness to perceive that even these three have merely cloaked their negative substance in a positive verbal disguise. The essence of every commandment — and every categorical imperative — is to forbid something; that which is forbidden is, in every case, a natural or vital process. Therefore: *the categorical imperative is the categorical annihilation of vitality.*

We advance to the ultimate proof of our contention. Every moral "you must" is directed against that which the moralist considers to be a "sin," thus the moralist always brandishes before the mind of man the concept of "sinfulness," or "wickedness." Without this concept of "sin," nothing would make the slightest sense to the moralist! The concept of sin covers, in fact, every "categorical imperative," every ethical demand, and every conceivable virtue (one can already see this happening in St. Paul). In the case of the animals, it is obvious that, since one cannot attribute the capacity for sin to them, they can commit no crime and will never be able to comprehend the claims of ethics. Life, therefore, knows nothing of sin; therefore, life is without sin and, hence, without guilt. We now ask, what is the peculiar significance of the Mosaic invention of sin? We hold the solution to that puzzle as soon as we realize that, according to the laws of the church, there is, in word and deed, only one "mortal sin," namely, the sin against the "Holy Spirit." The predicate "Holy" teaches us that the highest value, the *summum bonum*, the "supreme being," the *ens realissimum* of the ethical conscience is the spirit. Thus, there is only one genuine sin, the sin against the spirit! Now, as we have said, the spirit stands in opposition to life; therefore, what is considered to be sinful is life itself! From this quandary, no escape is possible. In order to understand an ethical "you must," I must first erect the concept of "sin," and in order to erect that concept, I must make spirit the measure of life, in such a manner, that life itself is directly connected with sin. And now we have arrived at the discovery of that truth which the teacher of ethics is hiding with his faith in the world-creating power of the commandment: the discovery that he himself stands in the service of a power that aims at the destruction of life; the ethical teacher is trapped, as it were, behind his spiritual barbed-wire, which mutilates life and sucks its blood; his mission is to poison his flock with the insane conviction of "sinfulness," and in order to achieve this end he must stuff the heads of his sheep with threatening fairy tales in order to contaminate and confuse their instincts. The teacher of ethics is nothing but the bloodless successor of inventive priests, and he will remain the advocate of negation forever and beyond. The priestly initiators may have been no more than a pack of ingenious con-men, but their followers are actually con-men who have managed to con themselves, con-men in all innocence, con-men with a good, even with the best — *conscience.*

A word has just escaped me that the ethical teacher always relies upon to bolster his case against me. He denies the "heteronomy" of the moral will of course, but he retains, on the other hand, the "autonomy" of his categorical "you must." He draws our attention back to the renowned "conscience," for he wishes somehow to make us believe that this conscience of his is part of man's constitutional endowment, and that it is an inalienable datum of man's inner life. Here, he is apparently saying: you would even disavow the "voice of conscience"; more, you would make yourself the advocate of every type of irresponsibility; you may even want to encourage every sort of wickedness and criminality!

On the contrary, we must ask *him*: if conscience is, in fact, a reality of life, why then is it not found anywhere else in the whole animal kingdom? If we wish to ignore the animals, is not primitive man in deep accord with the confirmed criminal in that neither has the slightest comprehension of the experience of conscience? How are we to doubt this fact? Shakespeare, who knew more about man than all of history's moralists put together, has his Richard III gloatingly aver that he has willed himself into becoming a villain! Shakespeare understood that the truly great villain never regrets the calamities that he has brought about; he only feels regret when he has failed to achieve his foul purpose. And where indeed can we find the conscience in such luminaries as Julius Caesar, Nero, Tiberius, Cromwell, Napoleon, and so on? As Goethe has said, "The businessman never has a conscience; at least, no one has ever encountered it." Accordingly, we revert to the erroneous view that conscience is an original fact of experience, and now permit ourselves to report our findings: the commander requires an obedient listener, otherwise his command amounts to nothing; the categorical imperative thus requires the existence of people who believe that such an imperative is sacred, or, more simply put, who believe that "Lord" Yahweh needs his slaves or else it is all over for his "Lordship." The ethical conscience certainly exists, for without it there could be no ethical teachers. But there also exists a power that is hostile to life, and this power loudly proclaims its presence in "conscience." So little substance, however, inheres in this conscience that is "common to all men," that we can dismiss those who are most deeply scarred by its stigma as "slave-men," which is precisely what Nietzsche calls them. How this "slave-man" arises will be, for those who have followed our exposition thus far, a simple question to answer: the "slave-man" has arisen, and he will arise, always and everywhere, as a result of racial bastardization and poisoning of the blood; and the slave-man has, as his necessary complement, the *criminal*. Thus, the student of life views the phenomenon of moralism as the spiritual expression of bad blood.

Since, however, it is a demonstrable error to consider the faith in duty as deriving from the sphere of life, we must at least point out that the instigators of moralism are lying when they attempt to persuade us that the amoral man, and the immoral one, represent the opposite of conscience, or even its absence. In fact, this false claim leads directly to the third allegation: that there is no conceivable system of values other than the ethical one, nor can there be. That, however, is irrelevant in view of man's status as bearer of spirit; in other words, one for whom the logical norm is by no means the ethical norm. As long as I only search for truth, discover truth, prove truth, I am ethically indifferent. But there exists, in opposition to the spirit's mode of evaluation, a value system which regards man from the standpoint of life. Just as the philosopher of spirit considers everything that denies spirit to be a "sin," the philosopher of life regards that which denies life to be an offense. The concept of sin sprouts from the same soil that nourishes ethics, but the concept of the offense has very different roots indeed. On this point, language dispels all doubt. Just as the moralist is completely bound by his dread of the sin against the spirit, so are we bound by our opposition to the offense against life. No one speaks of a sin against a tree, but men have certainly spoken in the past—and even today many still speak—of an offense against a tree. The tree neither is a spirit, nor does it house the spirit, and thus no one can commit a sin against it; nevertheless, the tree certainly lives, and therefore one can commit an offense against it. And just as the "sinner" must endure the destructive will of spirit when he experiences his ordained "punishment" in the midst of men, so is the offender against life punished according to the world-principle of retribution when he is confronted by the "vengeance of the Erinyes." The principle that embodies the offense against life is the categorical imperative. Therefore: *the ethical teacher is unconsciously a systematic offender against life.*

And so, therefore, we place opposite the forced denial of life an affirmative attitude. Accompanying the rejection of the offense must be a positive, caring attitude towards life. It is with some unease that I refer to this as education, because, as we have already seen, that word has already been pressed into the service of a moralistic sort of guidance for the soul. We will, however, employ the word education, provided the facts of the case are made clear.

No guide of the soul will ever be persuaded that he can change or improve anything at all. From the pine cone comes the pine tree, from the beechnut comes the beechtree, from the acorn comes the oak tree, and the guardian of the seed is neither its procreator nor the sculptor of its form. A plant does, nonetheless, require light and moisture, and the fortunes of the plant will depend to a large extent upon my caring for its needs. Thus, vital guidance for the soul lies not in the direction of the command and the promotion of the sterilizing faith in such threatening expressions as "you must." Vital guidance serves to provide the soul with sustenance. Had the expression "care of the soul" not been tainted by a parsonic aftertaste, there would be no better phrase to apply to the work of the esoteric soul-guide.

Where now do we find the mediators of the soul? We find them in wonder, love, and the example of heroes. The soul finds *wonder* in the landscape, in poetry, and in beauty. Thus, you look upon a landscape, a poem, or a thing of beauty, to see whether or not you can discover the beauty that flourishes therein. *Love*—in the broadest meaning of the word—entails reverence, admiration, and adoration: indeed, every type of heart-felt recognition that is warm and true, which can be evoked only by the beloved. The eternal icon that illustrates the soul's guide is embodied in the mother with the beloved child. The soul receives every shining ray of maternal love. The soul's *examples* are gods, poets, and heroes. The soul participates in the advent of the heroes when it delights in their shining shapes. And if you do not find that wonder, love, and example are flourishing within you, then it is your own inner life that is impoverished and no guide of the soul has the power to enrich you. For this is the secret of the soul: that it only grows richer by giving of itself. It is not the love that one receives that enriches the soul, but the love that is kindled within one through the receiving of that love. Thus, if you find that you are unable to arouse within your soul the secret wonders and the secret heroes, then the dazzling spectacle of the world would remain a mere theater production. Since your soul cannot respond, its guide will abandon you, and then you can sit yourself down and listen, unharmed, to—*a lecture on ethics.*

On Truth and Actuality (1931)

From time immemorial, the vexed question regarding a general criterion of truth has remained unanswerable, since any proposed solution would presuppose the validity of that which is in question. However, it is also unnecessary that we establish such a criterion, since there are numerous propositions, both factual and philosophical, that possess such inherently compelling force that we habitually refer to them as "immediately self-evident." Still, it is crucial that we understand that the expressions "true" and "false" pertain only to our judgments. In a world wherein there existed no thinking consciousness, such predicates would be utterly devoid of meaning.

Even if all of the discrete sciences should decide to coordinate their efforts so as to achieve one universal science that would be based upon correct and incontrovertible judgments, there would still be two opposed camps within that one scientific discipline when it came to the question regarding the actuality content of scientific judgments. The first group would explain as mere objects of thought that which the other camp would hold to be actuality itself; one group would see mere appearance in that which the other considered to be genuine substance. The one camp (which today constitutes the majority party) again falls into two sub-divisions, known as "idealists" and "materialists." The school of idealists, whose founding father is Plato, insists that the ultimate realities are concepts ("ideas," "representations"). The school of materialists, whose founding father is Democritus, holds that concepts are merely propositions that have been designed so as to correspond with objects. Above all, however, objects are objects of thought, which we comprehend with the aid of concepts: thus, both parties endorse the faith in the creative, or the formative, power of the (human) spirit, the idealist consciously, the materialist (for the most part) unconsciously. Therefore, we call the camp of the majority, comprising both the "idealist" and the "realist," the logocentric school.

The minority party, the party of opposition, we call the biocentric school. Its representatives look upon the matters in question as follows: all the proper objects of thought, both those mediated by thought and those immediately given, arise out of the sphere of actuality, but they do not contain actuality; for actuality can only be experienced, never conceived. Likewise, an understanding of the actual is certainly possible, but this understanding can never be exhaustively explained or conceptualized. The science of actuality is the science of appearances; the science of appearances strives to achieve a profound comprehension of the content of experience. Its aim is the discovery of that which Goethe referred to as "primal phenomena," in which the meaning of the world reveals itself.

Suppose that two individuals were successively to count the same one hundred dollars, and suppose also that one of the two had been born blind. Now these individuals' perceived images of the dollar bills would easily be distinguished from each other. However, that also holds true, if to a lesser degree, of the perceived images experienced by every living being; indeed, this also holds true of the perceived images in one and the same bearer of perception in different moments of his life. It follows that experiences can never be identically repeated.

In our judgments, we do not perceive reds or blues or colors as generalities; nor do we perceive sounds, tastes, and tactile sensations as generalities; nor do we perceive feelings of thirst or hunger, feelings of hope, yearning and expectation as generalities. What our judgments of the world do achieve, in fact, is this and this alone: we distinguish the multiform qualities, outer as well as inner, from each other. The qualities are thereby presupposed in the experiences. Our conceptions are derived from the qualities, since the conceptions are abstracted from the vital experience that is received. Whoever regards the objects of thought as actuality, confuses the boundaries that divide the objects with that which has established those boundaries. Conceptual thought must yield place to referential thought. The science of appearances, or the science of actuality, is the science not of conscious thought, but of referential thought.

In the major work of the author of these lines, *Spirit as Adversary of the Soul*, we present the proof of our contention that the objects of thought, both in the "idealist" and the "materialist" incarnations, cannot render the appearances according to their true nature. In every idealist philosopher we have a demonstration that the idealist's own principles render him incapable of distinguishing the world of perceptions from the world of representations. As a result, the idealist must perforce disavow the world of actuality; as a result, that world will always be found to play a miniscule role in the idealist's system. In fact, the idealist treats the world of perception as if it were a product of spiritual activity, whereas this activity could not raise itself up as the antithetical counterpart to the world of perception unless it had based itself upon a pre-existent substratum of vital events.

However, our experiences have no connection with the concept of being, nor have they any true relationship to the kindred concept of existence. For our experiences transform themselves without interruption; to employ the phrase of Heraclitus, they transpire in an "eternal flux." Actuality can neither be conceptualized nor quantified; only that being in which spirit subdues actuality can be thus rigidly fixed in concept and quantity.

As soon as one is convinced that the substance of experienced life is outside the reach of spirit, one is compelled to endorse the conviction that conceptualizing spirit, which is solely found in man, is a force that, in itself and for itself, does not belong to the cosmos. One can indeed marvel at the deeds that spirit, employing our activity, has consummated in this world; but one can nevermore fall into the error of attributing creativity to spirit. Spirit broadens the scope of man's will to power until we come to realize that spirit has at last unmasked itself as the will to annihilate nature. It is, thus, "utilitarian," and this is the reason why the "truths" of the party of spirit have seduced a greater number of disciples than can ever be found in the party of life. "Knowledge," in the biocentric sense, is seen as an end in itself. Such knowledge is only sought by the chosen few, who regard every glimpse into the nature of actuality as more rewarding than the fruits of utilitarianism and the will to power.

On the Problem of
Socrates (1918)

This cursory overview of our understanding of Socrates should be sufficient to prove that the alleged "problem" of Socrates was solved a long time ago. We confess that our standpoint is in marked opposition to prevailing beliefs; thus, our major emphasis will be placed on the pedantry and the sheer lack of creativity of Socrates. We will review the record thematically, and we will draw upon the opinions of clear heads of earlier times, so that with their assistance we will be able to present an unambiguous portrait of the character and the teaching of this most peculiar thinker.

There have been attempts to link the character of Socrates with a decisive turning point in the spiritual history of the Greeks; in large part, these attempts have misfired. Certainly, the unique importance of Socrates, that which has made him the most popular figure in the entire history of philosophy, lies, in any case, not so much in his doctrine as in his personality and his fate. He was not the founder of a religion, although he does invite comparison with certain earlier founders, as for example Pythagoras, in that Socrates, instead of crafting a *written* doctrine, attempted instead to bring about a change in the lives of his auditors through a *spoken* teaching that was religiously conditioned and morally tendentious. In a profound sense, he is the Greek world's unacknowledged forerunner of the Christian consciousness. Nietzsche goes so far as to attack Socrates as the instigator of the "revolt of the slaves in morality." With him there appears for the first time the unbounded self-mastery of a racially alien and, so to speak, international *rationalism*. He even referred to himself as a "citizen of the world." We are instructed in the Socratic teaching in part through Xenophon; in part through Plato, who situated an idealized representation of Socrates in his dialogues; and, finally, through the mockery of Aristophanes. Xenophon, who was, after all, an historian, may provide us with the most faithful account of the deeds and drives of Socrates; Plato, who placed his own doctrine in the mouth of his master, reveals to us, more critically than Socrates himself would have been able to do, the yet unknown aim of the Socratic direction of the spirit. In order to comprehend the specific meaning of the character of Socrates, we must focus our hindsight more closely on the life of this thinker than is the case with most other philosophers.

Socrates was born in Athens in 469 BC; he was the son of the sculptor Sophroniskos and the mid-wife Phainarete. He devoted his early years to sculpture, but he soon relinquished all vocational activity in order to develop a startling and unprecedented type of teaching career. He married a woman named Xanthippe who bore his children but who, as the result of his indifference to her, has unjustly received from the hands of posterity her reputation as the archetypal "shrew." In a word, Socrates was a professional guest, who spent his time engaged in endless discussions, in part with laborers, and in part, and above all, with attractive and cultured young men. The workshop, the gymnasium, and the drinking-bout were the favorite haunts of this amusing loafer.

With regard to the spiritual history of the Greeks in its general outlines, he would boast that he had never even made an attempt to study the doctrines of his philosophical predecessors, and, all things considered, Socrates presents the perfect picture of the half-educated, self-taught amateur, who, armed with the arrows of his naturally sharp critical sense and the acid of his plebeian mother-wit, upsets dull-witted men in general and the more highly educated in particular.

Even today, there are attempts to portray Socrates as a uniquely "harmonious" character. If we are not in error, Hegel was alone in disputing this error until Nietzsche, in his *Twilight of the Idols*, applied his unmasking technique to Socrates, thus providing, in its essentials, such a definitive demolition that no one reading it could have worn a more ironic smile on his face than — Socrates himself! To what extent his life-hostile doctrine deceived Socrates himself, it would be difficult to determine; but that he, thanks to his penetrating and all-dissolving, inner-directed rationalism, possessed an extraordinary understanding of himself, is almost beyond doubt, provided that there is at least some measure of truth in the stories that have been told about him. Thus, he is said to have responded to the remarks of a stranger who concluded, from an examination of the philosopher's face, that Socrates concealed every lust and every craving within his soul: "You know me well! But I have overcome them all." This proves that in no way did he consider himself to be a "harmonious" character, but rather a character who — to speak with Nietzsche — has become master over the anarchy of his drives, and who maintains his mastery by means of the clear light of rationality. We are also struck in no small way by what tradition tells us about his physical appearance. The rachitic, bulging eyes; the recessed, snub nose; the bald head and the pot belly must have made him appear hideous even to himself, for already during his lifetime, people had begun to compare him to Silenus. "Socrates," says Nietzsche, "belonged to the dregs of the populace, Socrates was rabble. One understands, one sees for oneself even now how ugly he was. But ugliness constitutes an objection. Among the Greeks, it amounted to a refutation. Was Socrates really a Greek?" In the Platonic dialogues much still shines through to indicate that aristocratic contemporaries of ancient racial stock saw Socrates in just this way. Aristophanes, in whose savage ridicule — perhaps! — the love of the ancient religiosity wages war with the self-seeking "enlightenment" of an already secular atmosphere, has, with sure instinct, in his comedy *The Clouds*, selected Socrates as the very embodiment of the vendor of sophistries; contemptuously, he says that, with dialectical fallacies as a foundation, the sophist's only purpose is to undermine tradition.

How did it come about that this character was surrounded by a halo in the eyes of the most talented young men of Athens? How could the Delphic Oracle have concluded that Socrates was the wisest of men? There were superficial grounds that may account for this judgment. Socrates manifested in the highest degree the quality that the Greeks called *sophrosyne*, which is equivalent to our notion of "self-possession." In modern terms, he was a thoroughly unemotional character, cautious and eminently cold-blooded. In certain respects, he anticipated the Cynics, who, like Socrates, were able to bear poverty, fatigue, and danger with an unruffled equanimity. He actually participated in many of the military campaigns conducted by Athens (Potidaea, Amphipolis, Delion), and, without the slightest trace of the "rush" of combat, he still maintained his iron courage on the day of battle. After a nocturnal drinking-bout, when the sprightliest among his young companions were overcome with wine, he would remain sober to the last, and, without a minute's sleep, he would head off to the Forum. This man was, in every moment of his life, the master of himself to such an extent that he embodied the very principle of his fencing mode of dialectic.

But he was also a great eroticist, and the novel style of his approach to young men was to endure throughout the rest of Greek history: the tendency to establish an erotic bond between an older man and a youth in the pursuit of *education*. From the time of Socrates, instead of the older lover, we have now the "master" and critic; and instead of the younger beloved, we have now the "student" and learner. This type of relationship had, in fact, long been the custom in Sparta; but, from the outset, the Socratic education no longer meant a teaching designed to develop *courage*, but one designed to develop that which Socrates called *wisdom*. Finally, Socrates was attended by a "presence," an apparition that we moderns might relegate to the precincts of "occultism." Periodically, an absent-minded, trance-like state would come over him, and it was said that he could become insensible for as long as an hour. At such times he would become oblivious to everything that was transpiring around him, and his stance became absolutely rigid. Then he would hear an inner voice that warned him to do this or that; sometimes he is given a serious task to perform, and at other times he is commanded to do something completely unimportant. He himself claimed that, without exception, the warnings were correct. In addition, the voice at times spoke, not to Socrates, but to one of his friends; and we have many instances in which the philosopher, thanks to this voice, avoided actions that, if he had performed them, would have led to disaster. Thus, he became accustomed to the promptings of a bright, visionary somnambulism, which, it was understood, strengthened the man who was under its sway.

Still, the astonishing vigor of its operation resides not so much within the "voice" as it does within the other party involved.

The soul of Greece was fragmented and exhausted when it gave birth to this nay-sayer who, like every prophet of dissolution, made his appearance in the guise of a "healer of souls." As we have said, Socrates was the complete master of himself; but he was more than that: he proved, or at least attempted to prove, that the assistance, not to say salvation, of which everyone stood in need, resided in the complete mastery of one's self. He claimed that such mastery is to be found in subordinating our uprooted drives to a detached rationality. He derided strong drives and an affirmative attitude towards life, and an impoverished and unsettled generation would have been startled at the forcefulness with which he announced his views.

Socrates knew exactly what he was doing when he embarked on the course that led to his own condemnation to death. As a living man, he had been the ruler of but one faction. As a martyr, he would conquer the world! In 399 BC the democratic forces which had just re-established their rule over Athens accused Socrates of "misleading the young" and "introducing new gods." At least the first and most important charge of the indictment was, as Hegel was the first to demonstrate, unimpeachable with regard to theory and perfectly in order with regard to practice. For we must bear in mind that among the dearest pupils of Socrates there had been Kritias, the bloodiest of all the Thirty Tyrants on one side, and, on the other, there was Alkibiades, who was responsible in large part for the crushing defeat, and attendant fall from power, of Athens in the disastrous Peloponnesian War. Socrates was found guilty, and had he now followed Athenian custom and requested a lenient sentence, he would undoubtedly have been let off lightly. Instead, he not only abjured every admission of guilt, but he even had the nerve to request that Athens bestow rewards upon him in recognition of the benefits that he had showered on the state and its youth! Certain now that their teacher would perish if he remained in Athens, his pupils arranged matters so that he would be permitted, without hindrance by the authorities, to escape his predicament. He categorically refused the offer: for he *wanted* to be executed, thus showing himself to be, once again, a forerunner of the Christian "redeemer."

Let us now begin to separate that which is fundamentally new in the Socratic teaching from that which can be dismissed as the stale wares of an epigone. In his own time, Socrates was judged to be the consummate Sophist. This judgment was certainly not intended to be a flattering one. He brought the hair-splitting dialectic and disputatious verbal jugglery of the Sophist to the pitch of perfection. The entire philosophy of the West has been encumbered ever since with this legacy. The sport of excelling by means of craft and the setting of snares (one side of which can be seen in the American mania for competitions) was first perfected by the Socrates who described himself as a philosophical "mid-wife." Likewise, he was a Sophist to the letter in his ceaseless war against traditional order and traditional morality; he was the self-mastering man who submitted all weighty matters to his personal conscience. However—and here we come to the truly new Socratic turning—it is not the personality that is made out to be the measure of all values, but solely that element of personality, which enables man to separate himself from the Cosmos in order to ascend to a "higher" rank: the spirit, reason, or, more accurately, the sense of rational purposefulness!

We have it from Socrates himself that the consideration of cosmological hypotheses left him cold. He utterly despised such modes of "speculation," and, because he was completely ignorant of the magnificent cosmologies that had been achieved by the hylozoists, he insisted on viewing the whole of nature entirely from the perspective of one who is only interested in its rational, practical applications.

The content of his philosophy is nothing but educational moralism.

The exposition of the Socratic *findings* must be subordinated to the exposition of the Socratic *method*, for it is not in the findings but in the method that his characteristic and unique contribution is to be found. Socrates employed a witty allusion to the vocation of his mother when he described his method as the *maieutic*, in other words, that of the midwife. He held the opinion that knowledge already slumbers in the soul of the student, and that it could be awakened solely through the employment of suitable concepts; thus, he sees his dialectical process, in a sense, as a birth. He was obviously denied the capacity to give birth himself in the natural fashion; but he says that he does have the modest gift that enables him to assist others to give birth — in the spiritual sense. The apparent modesty of this claim shows itself, on closer examination, to be rather startlingly arrogant. In the first place, Socrates insists that his opinion is to be accepted unconditionally by his students; but will it really be the opinion of his audience if it has managed to slumber within the listener to this very hour? In the second place, the entire procedure is presented as if, in fact, we are not concerned with the views of Socrates, or with any views under the Sun, but, rather, with something that is beyond doubt, something certain, that only waits to be discovered. There is already a sophistical trick here, which, for sheer cunning, puts all previous sophistical tricks quite in the shade, for we never discover just how this spiritual obstetrics is to be set in motion. On the first point, it is quite obvious that the Socratic claim cannot be demonstrated in the style of the earlier Sophists, who announced their views in well-prepared lectures, skillfully delivered; the Sophists really attempted to *persuade* their audiences. Instead of that, we get with Socrates a game of questions and answers, in which Socrates wards off all objections in the manner of the Japanese jiu-jitsu master warding off blows. Socrates never announces a proposition and defends his conclusion in statement and contradiction; instead, he causes the other speaker to advance judgments of his own. Socrates sees his first duty to be the refutation of such judgments. Placing the entire burden of proof upon the shoulders of the other speaker, Socrates easily demonstrates the untenable nature of the proofs that have been advanced by involving the speaker in absurdities. One may, perhaps, find that not everyone is inclined to follow this procedure of advancing propositions. In such cases, Socrates performs his unique trick. He stands silent; he laments that he still does not know what justice, virtue, and truth really are. He movingly begs the gods to teach him. This is the so-called Socratic irony; it is purely *verbal*, and, hence, a mere pretense. Soon a hesitant voice pronounces an opinion; in the blink of an eye Socrates is back at his dreadful and disputatious irony! Socrates is equipped with the perfect response to such fools as might ask additional questions: he has a hundred answers on hand. Every new answer unleashes ten new questions. The end is finally reached when the unlucky speaker lands himself in self-contradiction. The supposed knowledge was not real knowledge. At the beginning, Socrates was ignorant; the other speaker has shown him that he is even more ignorant than he had supposed. The first phase of the dialogue closes in an orderly manner, with this admission of ignorance. Now there begins the positive phase of the Socratic variety of mid-wifery, which, as we have already indicated, consists in bringing to conscious birth the knowledge that already exists within man. At this point in the proceedings, Socrates states that the other speaker's ignorance was actually a limited, or incorrect, knowledge of *himself*, and Socrates proceeds to assist in enabling the other speaker to attain to the correct understanding.

We now observe the results that follow from the formal side. Once again, we see that Socrates merely continued a scientific direction that had already been initiated by the Sophists. To wit, he proceeds by way of the analysis of concepts, or, more accurately, through analyzing the conceptual content of words. Although the Sophists had, in fact, employed this method, it constituted merely a secondary matter for them. With Socrates, it becomes the overarching priority, and thus there begins with him a new direction in the history of spirit. The Ionic hylozoists philosophized on the basis of the consciousness of the *object*; the Sophists on the basis of the consciousness of the *self*; Socrates, finally, philosophizes on the basis of the consciousness of *connection*: for him the concept is the spiritual bond that connects the object and the self (object and subject).

First, there is established, in the midst of a many-sided research program into linguistics, the exact analysis of semantics; second, there is an attempt to fix the conceptual boundaries of words, by defining them. The purpose of all Socratic dialectic is, after all, to make decisions that relate to concepts. It used to be said of Socrates that he cleverly planted in words opinions that he already held. But he provided a not inconsiderable epistemological service, for he was the first to open up the study of concepts, and therefore he can be said to have inaugurated a research trend for the Western world that has remained in operation to this very day. For the West, it is not so much the facts regarding the external world, but more the linguistic facts, that have been solidly established; thus, induction has won the day as our (questionable) conceptual mediator. It is readily understood that for Socrates, the designation of concepts is intimately intertwined with the discovery of truth. Nevertheless, the prevailing interest in all of the Socratic dialectic is the arousing of the soul of the listener: that is the true meaning of the Socratic *Eros*.

We ourselves have given some thought to the biological tendency exhibited in such a method, and our reflections have led us to the following conclusion: Socratism is founded upon a faith in the exclusive worthiness of conceptual thought (or consciousness). Regardless of whether an act was performed by a superior or an inferior person, the act can have no serious consequences so long as the person in question understands the motives for his actions; instinct, drive, and finally life itself are explained by Socrates as ignorance, and not, as with St. Paul, as sin. On the other hand, all good arises from (reflective) cognition. The Socratic method entails the Socratic findings, about which we will now have a few words.

Vice, sin, and deficiency of all sort, arise in error; virtue, excellence, and privilege are the results of correct insight (*Phronesis*). *Phronesis* can be taught, because its substance already resides within the soul of the erring person; but it is, as yet, only unconscious. Thus, virtue can be taught. Whoever attains to the correct insight, gains total possession of the self; he adopts a style of self-control that also enables him to hold himself accountable to that insight. This is done to achieve temporal as well as eternal blessedness (eudemonism). The Socratic ethic is, therefore, eudemonistic, but it is, at the same time, completely intellectual (the Kantian ethic is only the most recent model!). In its intellectualism, it establishes that it holds the primacy of virtue (or rectitude), in contrast to the Sophists, to be impersonal as well as universally binding; in its eudemonism, it remains utterly external, as this very principal ordains, because Socrates has told us that universally binding rectitude results in a completely practical purposefulness (aimed at attaining an even more absolute blessedness). Thus we revolve in an endless circle, for we are given no yardstick by which we can differentiate between a personal purposefulness and an impersonal one. It is merely a matter of formula when we are told that the true measure lies not outside us but rather within. Telling us that the true measure can be found within us remains the last word of the Socratic morality.

On "Psychoanalysis" (1928)

The so-called *psychoanalysis* (meaning analysis of the soul) is a bizarre bastard fathered by Herbart's atomism of representation upon Nietzsche's philosophy of self-deception. It is obvious also that the monstrous creature bears the impress of numerous other influences of a more exotic species, such as in the shape of the doctrine that the entire man, and, indeed, the entire world, is merely sex; or, to express it more moderately, that the living individual is a mere appendix to his genes, a variable dependent in relation to them. Proleptic glimpses of this notion are found already in the system of Schopenhauer, and its avatars were later cultivated by various biologists, who derived this notion from a doctrine that was espoused in earlier ages by physicians (certain scholastic doctors, for example, taught that *sperma virile*, if not spent, rises into the brain and there becomes spirit). However, this kind of theory should interest no one but the professional vulgarian, for it is certainly an unsubstantiated belief; a proof cannot even be attempted from the very nature of the case. (If, in accordance with this theory, the equation is set up, God = sex, then we have one of the main directions of the psychoanalytic propaganda; if the equation is reversed, sex = God, we have the other direction.) We need not pursue this any further.

From Herbart, whose tradition was never completely interrupted in Austria, we have received the idea of species of atoms of imagination which struggle for admission on the "threshold of consciousness," sometimes inhibiting and at other times potentiating one another; from Herbart we also receive the idea of *repression*; according to him, all strivings are due to instances of repression. When this idea was linked together with Nietzsche's view, which attributes a decisive influence upon the course of the activity of consciousness to the urges, and not least to the urges for self-esteem, a mythology of the so-called unconscious

arose to which we must allow the lure of the sensational, had not its
inventors been wholly afflicted with imaginative blindness. For this unconscious has a curious resemblance to a well-prepared defense lawyer;
its sole function is to use every kind of maneuver in order to persuade
consciousness to believe in whatever would be advantageous to the obvious, and even more to the secret, interests of the conscious entity, and
especially to shatter its belief in everything that might disturb his self-
esteem. Nietzsche's subtle and profound investigations of the tactics of
self-deception are here translated into a jargon that is appropriate to the
tedious office politics that may be studied in modern business life or in
the diplomatic ploys of our politicians. This method seeks a more prestigious status by calling itself "depth psychology."

But whatever may be the origin of all this, the psychoanalyst asserts that he is in possession of the truth, and points for confirmation
to the innumerable "cases" of which he disposes, meaning his patients.
However, two sides of the case must here be distinguished: the confes-
sion that the analyst elicits from the patient by means of an examination
that is based upon what he imagines to be so-called associations, and
successful cures by means of what is described by the precious word "ab-
reaction" [*Abreaktion*]. With regard to the confessions, the entire history
of psychoanalysis really spares us the proof that they either possess, or
can possess, any demonstrative force. At first, we all recall, the data obtained through this species of confessional were taken at their face value;
in other words, as being events that had really transpired in the life experience of the confessor. Later on, however, it was found necessary to take
them partly for fiction, although they might have a certain symptomatic
value; and today even this symptomatic value has undergone a change,
because it is clear that such confessions are often merely expressions of
how the "conscious" mind of the patient would prefer to see the meaning of his trouble (and hence himself) interpreted. But whatever is the
proportion of demonstrable events, of supplementary material, and of
unadulterated drivel, the insistent view that this method will lead to the
discovery of the etiology of the disease overlooks the fact that the source
of the disease is already presupposed as an x, if this confessional method
(which is often extended through years) is to be possible at all. Further,
it is necessary only to look more closely at any complicated example of
analysis to see that the meaning of the case, which the examiner requires for the validation of his doctrine, is imported by him, and that he
achieves success by virtue of a method which has the rare advantage that

it never fails: to the extent that the data that he elicits suit his view, he takes them literally; to the extent that they do not, he takes them meta-phorically, or, rather, as phantasms that have been substituted for wholly different contents of imagination. For this purpose he has prepared a system of a sexual symbolic language that, without exaggeration, can be applied to any single object in the universe. (For, after all, one can pigeon-hole every object in the universe as being convex or concave in *some* manner!) One must share this faith in order to believe in this kind of imaginary demonstration.

There remain, then, the cures. In order not to involve ourselves in endless digressions, let us examine them point by point:

1. If we possessed statistics of unassailable accuracy about all patients who were treated by psychoanalysis, we might become skeptical about these healers. Apart from a certain proportion of persons who were relieved of the disturbing symptoms, we would find a large proportion of those who ran away from their examiners, and no small proportion of those who were all the worse for the confes-sional. We are aware of most serious cases of this kind.

2. It is certain that these classes exist; but the proportions remain un-certain, for we do not possess statistics. We will therefore confine ourselves to the cures. We disregard the fact that in the treatment of every patient, but especially of a neurotic, the personal influence of the healer (whether he is a declared hypnotist, or homeopath, or internist, or psychoanalyst, etc.) plays an incalculable part. We also disregard the fact that psychoanalysis was fashionable for a time and still is so to some extent, and therefore, for reasons that will be easily understood, carries with it, in the eyes of the neurotic patient, an aura which assists the cure. On the other hand, it does something that would retain its curative value, even if all of the reasons that determine it were false: it gives the patient a full op-portunity for "having a good talk." Here it follows the approved methods of the Roman Catholic confessional.

3. In addition, it deals chiefly with hysterical patients. If we were right in saying that the hysterical type possesses abnormally small formative force combined with a highly developed desire to repre-sent, then it encourages him even to tell tales, to lie, and to invent; it affords him an opportunity of forming his inner life.

4. It affects something greater besides. Probably more neurotic types, and certainly all hysterical types, suffer from secret feelings of inferiority, although they are not always aware of this fact. Although the psychoanalytical confessional may be a plague, it offers him a ten-fold recompense by showing him new possibilities for taking himself seriously—very seriously—internally. Whatever crackpot notion or thought may creep through his consciousness, it is seen to be significant; it may even turn out to be an enchanted prince! A curious method, though nonetheless efficient, for strengthening self-esteem.

5. Psychoanalysis also has its secret, which, however, we are unwilling to publish, for perhaps it is effective only because the psychoanalysts themselves do not know it. Also, in order to reveal it, we would have to unfold the psychologist's psychology, which, though somewhat more entertaining than psychoanalysis, would also require a more lengthy exposition. If the author of these lines were a neurologist, he too would occasionally psychoanalyze his patients, and, perhaps, he too would be successful: not because he considers there to be any truth in the psychoanalytic chat, but because he holds that this prescription fits a contemporary variety of neurosis with amazing exactness. The two arise together necessarily, and will vanish together, for every epoch has its own neurosis, and no epoch that of another.

We trust that none of our readers will harbor the absurd suspicion that this effusion upon psychoanalysis is intended as an attack upon psychoanalysts. A genuine psychoanalyst cannot be refuted, and he is a fool who makes the attempt. It is true that there are many psychoanalysts who are not psychoanalysts at all. They do as Rome does—as the author, too, would do if he specialized in nervous cases. (In this matter the purse, too, can play a part.) But the real psychoanalyst—the man who holds the psychoanalytical worldview—is the true member of a religion, and as such cannot be assailed. If objections to personal immortality are raised before a strict Christian, he would not pay a moment's attention to them, but would ask himself what faults or even sins of the speaker prevented the light of the truth from illuminating him. If objections are raised before a true psychoanalyst, he does not attend to their value as proofs for a moment, but only asks himself what complexes or "repressions" (of sexual origin, of course) can be preventing the speaker from seeing and recognizing the light of truth — of *psychoanalytic* truth, that is. Predestination, beginning at the gene, determines the genuine psychoanalyst as it determines the genuine Christian. We therefore do not touch upon this matter; but we considered it proper to say a word about this scientific fashion, because we ourselves had an opinion to offer upon the nature of hysteria.

We would add expressly that there is one psychoanalyst to whom the above remarks about psychoanalysts do not apply unreservedly, namely, Freud. The man who founds a religion or initiates a new direction — and every direction has one initiator only — is of a very different stamp from his disciples, a fact which is not altered by feeble attempts at insubordination such as occur among all bodies of disciples: but Freud is a pioneer, and if any part of his work should survive, it will be associated with his name, and with his name alone. If he believes in the doctrine of psychoanalysis, he does so because he made, or, if it be preferred, created it: and although a pioneer can neither be taught nor converted, it requires no common degree of simplicity in order to confuse his obstinacy with that of a disciple. The psychology of the pioneer is of a different class, and does not here concern us. But we would say that this man has some of the true speculative spirit, together with temperament and stubborn tenacity. Unfortunately, he has an inferior soul and a narrow horizon. This is to be regretted for other than merely practical reasons, for such thoroughbred energy might have been expected to make real, and not only *imaginary*, discoveries!

On Academic Psychology
and Characterology (1928)

The following reflections have a certain significance in the history of psychology; the scholastic methods of psychology that are here criticized still persist in wide circles even after the passing of many years: for these reasons we state what bears upon these points in much the same shape as before.

Suppose one were to ask of psychology what would be the minimum of knowledge to which it ought, in fairness, to offer a key: for example, what has been the nature of the change in mind since the Classical period; the distinction between civilized and "natural" man; of what vital facts the ruling religions, the various castes, and the different races are the index; what constitutes a statesman, a priest, a strategist, artist, or scientist; what are the laws which govern jealousy, greed, or selfishness; how to lay hold of a man's enduring characteristics behind his changing actions, and how to lay hold of the true motives behind the mask of his politeness: suppose that these or similar questions were asked, then the inquirer would only be disappointed by the tendency of our day. He will undoubtedly come to the conclusion that he has been asking in the wrong quarter. For, to his disappointment, he would hear of sensations, perceptions, imaginations, judgments, strivings, acts of will, feelings — in short, of the commonest characteristics of mental existence, or of the nature of our organs of sense (the admirable nature of whose physical structure is not disputed). He would be instructed in the method whereby conclusions are drawn; how something is remembered; and how concepts are formed. His study of history, law, or religious consciousness, of the forms of mental sickness, or his interest in understanding practical life would be enriched, but little more than would be the botanical studies of a lover of flowers who might be instructed that these are spatial bodies fixed in their places, capable of growth, requiring certain food, and dependent upon light.

We do not desire to combat modern psychology and its openings (some of which show promise): the more so, as we shall invoke its assistance successfully more than once in the course of our argument. But, for reasons that will be touched upon later, it is certainly not what its etymology implies it to be: for it is not a science of *soul*. Nevertheless, we are fully aware of what modern psychology has accomplished, and of the analytical training, hitherto perhaps without parallel, which it introduced. In this connection the name of Theodor Lipps must be recalled. Quite undeservedly he has been forgotten, and in fact it is a difficult matter to do justice to this thinker. Of the results that he obtained, hardly anything remains, apart from some discoveries about the observation of space and the psychology of metrics. He had a tendency to view actuality as the phenomenal manifestation of a transcendent "world-ego," a tendency that bears the imprint of the reigning liberalism of the 1860s, and so restricts his vision in such a way that one is tempted to say that it is bounded by his desk. But within a horizon that, so to speak, is spaceless, he has an eye of microscopic power, and this eye is actually turned inwards. If the *Psychologie* of Wundt, with all of his reading, is compared with any of the works of Lipps, it will be abundantly clear after a perusal of a few sentences that the latter practiced genuine psychology, even if it is no more than the analysis of the contents of consciousness, while the former practiced everything under the Sun, but never psychology. (To put it somewhat forcibly, one might say that Wundt's psychology consists in the fact that he tosses in the adjective "psychological" half a dozen times on every page.) In short, although his world-view has already been forgotten, Lipps alone — so far as we can see — among the popular professors of the last generation was enabled by his method of self-examination to anticipate and prepare a way for the study of appearance, which now has once again become practicable. In order to give a name to his merits in this connection, however, we would recall that it was he who, with an accuracy hitherto unattained, taught how to distinguish that connection of facts of consciousness to which self-reflection bears witness and, again, their demonstrable dependence upon the peculiar characteristics of the conscious entity, from that causality by whose aid we make calculable the sequence of processes in the world of things.

At any rate, he prepared an explanation of the assumption of causality by applying a certain manner of experiencing to extra-spirituality, namely, that of the activity of the will that causes action (his *Bewusstsein und Gegenstände* is especially valuable in this regard).

However, we feel that the time has come to remember that the course upon which modern psychology as a whole has entered never leads beyond a somewhat restricted range of questions; that it is possible to treat its subject by other methods; and that it runs the risk of exposing itself dangerously if it persists in raising those foolish objections to a loftier conception of psychology, the commonest of which will be disposed of now.

Under the influence of the curious belief that its favorite concepts — that sensations, imaginations, feelings, and the like are the psychically simple data — the atoms, so to speak, of which the mind is properly composed — psychology believes that it ought to reject as premature and unscientific any dealings with questions of characterology. We do not now ask whether it was ever seriously hoped to solve the problem that lies, for example, under the name of Napoleon, by analysis of processes of thought and of the commonest estimations of value. The objection in any case is invalid. For nothing is less immediately "given" to observation than the fact, simple enough in the meaning of modern psychology, of the perception of *red*. A red ball a yard distant from my eyes appears very different to a child and to an old man; to myself when rested and when tired; to instantaneous and to protracted observation; to a hungry and a full man, or to a merry and a sad one; it appears different under changing illumination, and if placed before a white, green, or red background; quite apart from the fact that unconscious — if not conscious — comparison is required in order that the same or even a similar redness shall be recognized in a raspberry, the evening sky, red wine, blood, a brick, a tiger lily, and a coral. Redness, and even a redness more closely determined, is a structure of thought; it is extracted through the elaboration of contents of perception, but it is not itself a content of perception; and whatever we might succeed in establishing with regard to the perception of red, it would never furnish us with a brick with which to build personality.

But even if it were a conceivable task to translate personality into the language of such universal concepts as must be developed in order to elucidate the processes of perception, this would still demand the closest acquaintance with personality. Once we possess this, we may perhaps be able to derive peculiarities of personal color perception, and to test experimentally the correctness of our conclusions; otherwise we look for them in vain from any theory of color perception, however perfect. The case is similar to that of cytology, for it is certain that most of the processes with which that science deals belong to categories which are proper partly to physics and partly to chemistry, but which are much more complicated, from the standpoint of those sciences, than any chemical processes known to us. Here, too, then, a warning might be made against the study of cells on the ground that chemistry is not yet sufficiently advanced in order to cover with its formulae all the phases of germ-formation, cell division, and so forth. Fortunately, man's search for knowledge has disregarded such out-of-date impediments: with the best results, it has made the cell the center of a science of its own, which even now toys with a resurrection of the *vis vitalis*.

The concept of a cell can be defined as exactly and unambiguously as that of light, sound, heat, magnetism, chemical affinity, and so on; and it demands to be considered independently, because it appears as the medium of those innumerable processes the totality of which we call life, and which we must know before we can undertake their interpretation in terms of physics.

A comparison of the cell with the soul seems relevant in more than one sense. Like the cell, the soul is the substratum of certain processes of the inner life, of which the modern analysis of the facts of consciousness reveals little more than would be revealed of the life of a cell by a consideration that should demonstrate in it the laws of physics and of chemistry. Naturally the concept of a cell, like that of character, is reached through abstraction. But it would appear inconsistent with natural thinking to use the vital processes merely to illustrate chemistry, and similarly it must cause surprise and even amazement that the "science of the soul" does, in fact, do something quite similar, in neglecting all the qualities of character, and eliminating the nature of the substratum, and finally allowing validity only to those which remain as differential signs of mental existence. We ask with astonishment how it was possible, before making any attempt at the exploration of character, to proceed towards that maximum of abstraction that was so hostile to man's original interest in man. This remains to be explained later, and we now already remark that the unnatural direction of this development is the reason why the science of psychology and the soul-skilled wisdom of all times and peoples are strangers to one another today. Although the former direction may perhaps be justified, the latter is still closer to real life; a deeper need requires it and it admits of an unlimited progress. The dangers that threaten a scientific treatment of its material, as opposed to the objections that we have refuted, are due to the inclination to plant the ruling notions in the ground that is to be freshly ploughed. But here we touch upon, and negate, certain instructive excrescencies of modern psychology.

The more it was believed that unanimity existed about the fundamental facts of consciousness, the more attention was paid to the differences which must, in the nature of things, subsist in the capacities of individual minds for imagination, apprehension, striving, and the like. It was hoped to effect a reversion of the process, and to construct a kind of individual psychology from permutations and combinations of the universal characteristics. But here it appeared, as was inevitable, that the crucial question was unknown, and that the means for solving it were lacking. First, it was overlooked that it is not the distinction in these processes (a distinction which is generally unimportant) that is the goal of investigation, but the permanent disposition, which may be discovered through the distinction, but not through it alone. At this point a new branch of psychology was hatched that bore the name of "differential psychology," which is about as reasonable as to call cytology a differential chemistry, or optics, acoustics, and thermics, a differential mechanics! A wrong track was inevitably reached, which led not to personality, but through a weary waste of its *disjecta membra*, scattered abroad (so to speak) in the shape of degrees of sensitiveness, operations of association, comprehension, of observation, combination, judgment, and reactions—showing no law which might unite them, and still less the "spiritual bond."

At the same time the experimental method, whose validity in the mental sciences is generally open to doubt, was applied to the sphere of characterology, where it is entirely useless. The inevitable constraints even in neutral experiments for testing perception, judgment, and reaction may modify the mental disposition of the medium and invalidate the result; all security must vanish when it is no longer permissible to neglect the peculiarity of the object, since it is precisely this uniqueness that is to be ascertained. (French investigators made their own contribution to the confusion when they meticulously avoided the traditional nomenclature; they then made the grand discovery, based on descriptions given by pupils of pictures shown to them, that there are some four types of apprehension: the descriptive type, the observational type, the emotional type, and the learned type!) It must, moreover, be considered whether experiments can ever teach us what we ought to know first of all—whether a man is envious, covetous or devoted, whether faithful and true or capricious and flighty, whether of a happy disposition or gloomy, brave or cowardly, bold or timid—and what is the nature and operation of these and similar qualities.

The wrong formulation of the question produced a corresponding fiasco all along the line in the results—which we would pass over in silence, but for the fact that it seems more fitted than any other datum to reveal the traditional limitations of the modern handling of psychology. We select as our example no obscure light, but an authority rightly acknowledged by everyone. Kraepelin is a student who must be treated with great respect in his special field of psychopathology; he is also a master of the art of clinical classification. As fundamental qualities of personality he posits capacity for training, for stimulation, and for fatigue. (More exactly, we would present the following categories: capacity for performance, for practice, for retention of what is practiced, special memory, capacity for stimulus, for fatigue, for recovery, depth of sleep, capacity for distraction and for habituation.) That is, the difference, for example, between Diocletian and Gregory VII must be reduced to differences in capacity for training, stimulation, and fatigue! Criticism is superfluous.

From this, not only is its fundamental estrangement from the facts of life of this kind of thought obvious, but also its particular interest. The question here is not the qualities of personality, but the inner causes of its effectiveness. And even effectiveness is not estimated in its totality, for if it were, then initiative, inventiveness, intuition, and everything else that borders on the sphere of creative impulses would have to be investigated: here the only quarry is the conditions of one's ability to work; as indeed is proper to an age which has long grown unaccustomed to the view of great individualities, and has replaced nobility of blood by the dubious honor of professional fitness. Man, as such, is no longer seen or known, but is only an intellectual mechanism, the servant of an external purpose, and having for its criterion a hypothetical "end."

This end was unknown to other ages. A Renaissance busied with psychology might perhaps have considered a man's faculty of action as worthy of investigation; a Medieval period, the strength of his faith; a Classical period—in part, at least—his capacity for happiness. Such traits have lost their value for the modern psychologist; they are not even regarded at all, and industry has remained as the only virtue, accompanied by its satellites, ambition and success—a complex, that is, which the Greeks and Romans would never have hesitated to relegate to the lowest of men, to pariahs and to slaves.

Others may applaud an advance to austerity: this is certain, that science should remain neutral, and turn a deaf ear to the suggestions of an ochlocratic idealism. But instead, it is completely hypnotized by the latter's standards of value, and the practical nature of its apparatus is completely in harmony with a tendentious partiality in the impulses which point the way. But this does not apply to psychology alone, but to all of the philosophy of the last centuries, insofar as it is attached to names traditionally famous. The development, briefly, was as follows.

After the Reformation had undermined Mediaeval piety, morality appeared as the true kernel of Christianity, and now it appears to be more potent than any idolatrous form of superstition. From it, not only all systems since the beginning of the modern period received a moral tincture—atheism most of all—but it also governed the exploration of the facts of the natural and mental sciences, which to this day denies, neither in method nor in results, its origin from the Christian dogma of the kingdom of God. But spirituality without metaphysics becomes a faith in reason and finds itself referred, both in truth and in error, to the two foci of logic and utility—otherwise known as the "good."

We do not, of course, here follow the development of rationalism, or the belief in the essential rationality of the world-process; which would mean to write the history of spirit from a wholly novel point of view; we only mention what is essential for an understanding of the development of psychology. After the first assault of mechanistic thought, which was naturally directed against the universe, and won those great conquests of physics (Copernicus, Galileo, Kepler, Huyghens, Newton) which the nineteenth century could do no more than to perfect, there followed a self-reflection of the organ of thought, mediated by the question of the range of the use of understanding and the reasons for the inviolability of its results. The self-analysis of reasonableness, which sometimes took a speculative and dogmatic, and sometimes a purely analytic turn, was given the somewhat too narrow name of "critique of cognition"; and, since Kant, no small credit was taken for a renunciation of metaphysical desires. Now modern psychology in all of its manifestations is a particular form of this critique of cognition. Its object is not man, but rational man, in other words a being which can *think logically* and *act in a utilitarian manner*; and the mainspring of its investigation is not an interest in life—which is the proper province of psychology—but in the capacity for thinking and willing—which is that of logic.

But in view of the singleness of its fundamental aim, it is of little importance whether it finally masters its tasks with or without "soul," whether it attributes great or little importance to the gray matter of the cerebral cortex, and whether it clings to experiment or devotes itself to the art of definitions. Among the unpleasant results, we shall always find an amazing ignorance of the urges and passions which, as "lower," are hardly considered worthy of notice; helplessness in the face of the unconscious, or the psychical substratum even of reasonable actions, of which for years we learned nothing save the vague "laws of association"; uncritical acceptance of moral judgment, which at the least encourages a superficial classification; a foolish misinterpretation of every unsocial human type as a differential form of unnatural "freak"; and complete failure before the problem of individuality or the inner multiplicity of times, peoples, castes, strata of culture, and of everyday life. In part, it commands respect for its achievements in its critique of cognition and its masterly analysis of the processes of apprehension, but it appears as the sickly offspring of average common sense when it is taken as what it professes to be—a science of the inner life. The entire achievement of the so-called "science of psychology" in this respect is outweighed by a single page of Goethe's or of Jean Paul's; and it is impossible to evade the bitter truth which Novalis had already pronounced when he says that this so-called psychology is one of those false idols which have usurped that place in the sanctuary where the true images of the gods should stand.

But even today the "inner life" is somewhat deeper than it appears in the mirror of psychology, and consequently it gives individual impulses to the investigating mind which lie beyond its general considerations: in reality, therefore, it has not achieved the first thing which might rightly have been asked of it: to establish a critical foundation of the "sciences of the spirit." Philology, historiography, ethnology, psychiatry, and practical knowledge of mankind alike looked to it for help in vain—as was shown at the beginning—and therefore in time a new treatment of the material must come to the front which, while retaining the more exact knowledge of the processes of cognition, makes it its task to understand the whole wealth of forms of the life of the soul.

But such a treatment lacks neither precedent nor yet a certain tradition, even if we neglect the sages of all times and peoples who never practiced psychology in the intellectual sense. The impulse of psychological investigation is most active in that epoch of German spiritual life that is called *Romantic*, whose later period contains the name of the physician and thinker Carl Gustav Carus. It suffices to mention this name, which, though not the greatest, yet denotes a man in whose nature the roaming element of those days found a caution prudent enough to allow it to condense into a doctrine that still awaits elaboration and extension, instead of exhausting itself in prophetic imaginings. But the research of Carus, and similar essays of contemporary minds, together with many fruitful germs of the 1830s and '40s, was swept away by the course of development, so that now the chain must be linked afresh and across a gap of time.

But all this could not be done with so sure an eye for every elective affinity without the mighty achievement of that man of the most recent past whose coming, even if it allows of no new hope, still crowns the decline of man with a proud luster—the achievement of Friedrich Nietzsche. Reasons, the analysis of which would here lead us too far afield, cause the ardor of metaphysical intuition to feed the stream of criticism in him almost exclusively, giving it a piercing quality never reached before. The instrument of his prophetic power is the gift, armed with the arrows of acutest understanding, of "discrimination of spirits." For the first time since the Middle Ages, and in the more familiar forms of the most immediate present, he furnishes us with an example of that millennial flower, the great piercer of souls and reader of spirits, who, unlike the poets, does not bury under flowery meadows of fanciful sentiment the outlines of fire-born truths. It would require a separate section, if justice were to be done to his significance for a possible future psychology. (We have since written a whole treatise on this subject: *Die psychologischen Errungenschaften Nietzsches*, J. A. Barth, Leipzig.) Here we merely state a fundamental fact, and now pass over to the next discussion by designating the essentially psychological attitude by that symptom which emerges most clearly, especially with Nietzsche.

The real scope of his philosophy is the devaluation not only of ethics but, further, of intellect, of which, for the first time in the known "history of the world," paradoxically enough, the disposition, that is, in this case, the *biological* value, is scrutinized, without prejudice or favor, by the eye of spiritual hostility. "That it is false is no objection to a judgment"—a proposition the consequence of which may be followed in its more positive counterpart—correctness alone does not make a judgment valid, truth is no value in itself. Even the organ of thought, whose mainsprings are reasons and causes, proves to be conditioned by its urges, and its criteria are subjective. It is possible to side for or against logic, and (this is Nietzsche's most important application) the latter is done when we take the side of life, which is unspiritual and non-logical. Life and spirit are distinct, and, as Nietzsche apprehends it, spirit is a diseased form of life.

It is possible to take a further step, and this will be done in the chapter which deals with the metaphysics of the distinctions of personality: and, although the shattered autonomy will be restored, this will be done only to widen the gap until it becomes the fundamental dualism (which appears as a necessity of thought) between life (element, soul) and spirit. In fact Nietzsche continually makes use of this, although he still takes spirit as a by-product and tries to treat it too anthropocentrically—as derailment and *lusus naturae*. Before him, there was no student of the soul whose analysis, however subtle, did not end with a new "rehabilitation" of man; for example, even the methodical skepticism of Stirner has for its ultimate pole an ideal of personality which (although alien to most) might be described as the "domination of the consciousness of uniqueness." Nietzsche, on the other hand, takes up his position outside man, or, in the most literal manner, "beyond good and evil," as is evidently fitting in one who makes man the object of his study. In this way alone he was able to unmask the envy of life (resentment) at the roots of every moral judgment and to lay bare the atrophy of instinct which, in the guise of numerous "ideals," distorts the view of man—especially of modern man—when he looks upon the world.

We must stand opposed to that which we would understand; this is a necessary condition of all cognition, as the name object itself irrefutably proves. We remain within the metaphor (which in fact is more than metaphor) if we add that the survey is hindered if the object is too close and that philosophy rather demands a "distance"; however little we may like a name that, since the time of Nietzsche, has become a favorite with writers. For proximity fixes the eye upon one point and isolates the object of this contemplation at short range; it leads inevitably to that atomism of thought which was exemplified by the scholastics; whereas distance, as it widens the horizon, demands, so to speak, a roving eye, which opposes to the belief in the isolated entities of the objects the totality of an image.

We emphasize the meaning of the word "intuition" as a kind of cognition that is cognate to contemplation; next, there follows the "world-view," which has now become somewhat rarer. The image, or vision, alone rises to the acid test of attention, and compels the spirit with an irresistible force of conviction. But distance causes the incomplete actuality of objects that have been merely "focused" to plunge back into a totality of contemplation; consciousness, whose eye merely *distinguishes* in the light of common day, borrows from it something of the *synthetic* foresight of the prophetic eye. The profundity of truth varies with the seeing power of the spirit that seeks it.

The study of the soul concerns itself with facts that in themselves are non-sensuous; the individual finds within himself the material needed in order to interpret them. Consequently the spirit must be able to achieve a relation of exteriority in order that it may experience the personality of which it is a part; in one sense it must dehumanize itself in order to look upon this human quality precisely; and it must even have the skill to remove itself so far from it that the individual traits of the inner life coalesce into an image for it, whence it may read partial characteristics as the corporeal eye reads the position of a particular place on a finished map. But images, whether they be dreamed or perceived, are spatial-temporal actualities. Consequently we state the facts more exactly in saying conversely that a gift for studying the soul rests essentially upon a capacity for seeing its meaning in the phenomenal world. But to see the "meaning" in it means *to see the phenomenon symbolically.* And, indeed, it is an implicit trait of the philosopher's vision, which it shares with that of the artist and poet, that, following an irresistible compulsion, it apprehends things symbolically: herein (in spite of the enormous difference) it resembles the spiritual disposition of the "savage."

Now it is not only the fascinating, but also the essentially true element in Nietzsche's mental attitude, that he thus sees individual persons as well as entire peoples, cultures, and epochs according to the analogy of pictures. For example, he speaks of the "Nordic gloom" of "haunting thought and thin blood," he calls the southern soul "an abundant fullness of Sun and irradiation of Sun," and discovers "clumsiness and peasant gravity" in the Englishman: in short, he uses convincing traits of its sensuous appearance to stamp each character, or rather he finds in the visible world the key to the invisible, and draws from the actuality of the symbol its conceptual element.

Formulated as a principle, this means that we must have the whole before we can successfully undertake to study the parts. It is possible, of course, to analyze the former into the latter, but to compose the former out of the latter is impossible, unless the idea that is to guide the process of composition has already been extracted from the whole. New and fruitful thoughts always arise at some point of that profoundest dividing line of the spirit where the symbolism of phenomena ends, and they begin to be symptoms. The Romantic philosophy is wholly dominated by the symbol — by the fact, if not by the concept. The world is taken as a vast symbolic language, which must be deciphered by speculative absorption; we do not observe facts, but look upon their face and ask what vital pulse, what secret constructive impulse, or what evolution of the soul seems to speak in these lines. The doctrines of the growth of plants or of crystals or of the motions of the cosmos are treated as a kind of physiognomics of the universe; and conversely Carus, characteristically enough, gives the name of "symbolism of the human form" to the physiognomy of man in the title of his chief work on that subject.

This leads us to revert to the importance of the image as a starting point for the study of the soul. In the sense that has been laid down by us, this must primarily be a morphology, or doctrine of the forms, of the soul's anatomy. But forms in the proper sense are external forms, and no science of the inner life could afford to renounce to be guided by its sensuous manifestations without risking a lapse into amateurishness. We consider the psychological manner of contemplation as not only cognate to the physiognomical, but as fundamentally identical with it. The new intuition, whether reached by the most circumspect thought or by lightning illumination, always has its source in an extension of an understanding of the symbolism of the external world, or in the progress of the spiritual assimilation of physiognomies hitherto alien. However, we have thus given a shape to the contrast between our own and the traditional point of view that, detached from its place in the logical sequence, would appear as capricious paradox. We therefore meet an impending misunderstanding, and end by throwing light upon this formula (which in truth must be taken literally) from another side.

A special effort on the part of modern students was needed in order to master the heresy that our knowledge of the inner life is increased by investigation into the nervous system. No more than twenty years ago it was seriously believed that a study of the anatomy of the brain afforded instruction in psychical processes. In proportion as this unphilosophic hope vanished, "pure" psychology grew up by the side of "physiological" psychology, and the provisional thesis of the "psychophysical parallelism" established itself. Our demand that the psychical is to be construed out of its phenomenal form might therefore be misinterpreted as constituting a relapse into a direction to which "pure" psychology stands much closer. For it is not of essential importance that we shall discuss extra-sensual facts in a preponderantly physical, or, on the other hand, in a preponderantly psychological language: the only question is whether such concepts have, or do not have, their origin in a view of the totality of the organism. Ganglia, nerves, the convolutions of the brain and the like are, within the body, only *disjecta membra*, so to speak, as, in the sphere of the inner life, are perceptions, imaginations, processes of sensation, and so on. The symbolism of the body is so far from coinciding with any concepts of the anatomy of the brain that the latter must be completely forgotten if we would reach the former. The soul does not reside in the brain, but in the form, and, if a paradox were permitted, we would recommend in place of a study of man's nerves, a study of his *superficies*. We will conclude with a sentence of Novalis, who anticipated the truth here as he so frequently did elsewhere: "The seat of the soul is at the point of contact of the inner and the outer world."

On Consciousness and Life (1915)

The word "consciousness" is customarily understood as having a double meaning: first, the substance, or content, of experience; and second, the critical empiricism which observes that experience. In experience, we occupy a station *within* consciousness, whereas during the process of empirical apprehension, we stand *outside* experience. The first state possesses actuality for itself (*für sich*), whilst the second state can be said to approach actuality only insofar as it remains connected to the first. Life has no need for the process of comprehension in order to exist, although spiritual comprehension does require the presence of a living "event" (*Geschehen*) in order to commence its operations. Bearing these reflections in mind, it is of fundamental importance for the theory of consciousness that we indicate precisely which of the dual meanings is under examination. Ordinarily the word seems to suggest — for instance, as it is employed in the substantival infinitive of the declaration: "I am conscious of myself" (as of an object) — that it actually refers not to an *object*, but, rather, to an *observation*, and it certainly piques our interest to discover that current scientific terminology, in heart-warming conformity with popular usage, has endorsed the latter interpretation exclusively. Unfortunately, this approach excluded consciousness itself from consideration so thoroughly that the whole structure of psychology almost seems to have been established upon a false fundamental principle, a procedure that would certainly entail ominous consequences for such derivations as had been drawn from it. But before we continue to develop our exposition, it is necessary that we now interpolate a brief digression.

Even if consciousness should be equated with spiritual comprehension, there would still be two distinct modes of non-consciousness: utilizing the terminology of contemporary thought in the narrow sense, these modes are the *unconscious* and the *unobserved*. Several instances, among the dozens that are available for our perusal in the relevant literature, may enable the reader to appreciate certain distinctions. No one possesses an instantaneous (immediate) consciousness of everything that he has ever learned, although certain items exist "unconsciously" in a state of readiness until, in response to a suitable question, they "enter into consciousness." This provides the conclusive explanation of one of the inherently fascinating phenomena in the field of characterology, namely, our undergoing an experience that is apparently of the "unconscious" variety, only thereupon discovering that it has been, as it were, "deposited" in consciousness in a procedure analogous to a routine cash transaction at a banking institution. It is a somewhat different case when we have an instantaneous, or immediate, experience, although, paradoxically, we are unable simultaneously to observe that which we have just, in fact, experienced. Example: in reading a suspenseful novel, a person may, so to speak, "turn a deaf ear" to the clock's striking of the hour even though the clock is in the near vicinity; with the reader's consciousness focused so intently upon the story that he has had no time to observe that, while he was reading this novel, his feet became ice-cold. Nevertheless, he has certainly undergone both experiences. It might happen that our reader subsequently discovers that he can recall the clock's striking of the hour. He thereby achieves some comprehension of an experience that he has hitherto attempted to explain to himself in vain. Let us glance at another paradox: the more an event moves us emotionally, the less we are competent to observe our condition as it is *in itself*; for one "forgets oneself," to use a profound turn of phrase, out of concern, out of dread, or out of an excess of stormy bliss. With this brief survey, we are now sufficiently prepared to ponder one more puzzle, but this time we will draw our material from the area of world history, in order to precisely demonstrate the extent to which the concept of consciousness itself has served as the source of an endless proliferation of erroneous doctrines.

We do not err in tracing the birth of our modern intellectual tradition to the renowned formula of Descartes: *cogito ergo sum*. It would surely violate the intentions of its creator were we to translate this proposition as "I think, therefore I am," without certain qualifications. We have, in fact, generally understood the Cartesian *cogitare* to comprise not merely the act of thinking, but also such activities as perceiving, feeling, willing, and even dreaming: in brief, we have come to regard the *cogitare* as the equivalent of consciousness in general. Still, there can be no doubt whatever that, in this regard, the philosopher had in mind not only perception, representation, and emotion, but also the *perceived* phenomenon, the *represented* image, and the *empirically observed* emotional state. However, the thinker who has seen the decisive act of consciousness in critical comprehension, will, of course, be quite prepared to champion the proposition: "mind is thinking substance" (*mens est res cogitans*). But Descartes (on grounds the comprehensive exposition of which would lead us deeply into the evolution of the human spirit) stumbles badly in his treatment of this line of thought due to his inability to study these discrete entities separately; as a result, he necessarily confuses our *consciousness* of experience with *experience itself*, and Descartes has thereby allowed himself, as well as all succeeding posterity, to get bogged down before a Cartesian roadblock. This impediment has, in effect, barred the approaches to a fresh, sense-oriented philosophy of life ever since.

We have always considered the most startling aspect of the Cartesian formula to be the precedence that it accords to the self before the object. The philosopher discusses consciousness as if he were analyzing the content of experience, whereas what he is really doing is formulating critical judgments *about* experience. Thus, the faculty of judgment usurps the place of experience, and the upshot is that Descartes has effectively sacrificed the entirety of man's inner life to mere cognition. With that superb logical consistency that was ever the hallmark of his thought, Descartes explicitly announces the inescapable consequences of his philosophical meditations: the whole world is to be reduced to the status of a nexus of quantifiable physical forces; animals are to be regarded as nothing but soulless machines; and the stirring emotions that characterize the nature of man are to be dismissed as *perturbationes animi*! Such frank admissions could hardly have failed to rouse the ire of a host of passionate enemies. But even the bitterest foes of the Cartesian philosophy endorsed their antagonist's pseudo-antithesis of *cogitare* and *esse*, and once they had made this false start, they merely contested the predominance of consciousness over being in a procedure as fruitless as any counter-claim that arrogates to being the predominant rank as the foundation of consciousness. Thus the bitter strife continues to deepen between the two ancient camps of metaphysicians, the "materialists" and the "idealists," behind whose inviolable fortress-walls, one might almost persuade oneself, an evil genius of deceitful plots to imprison the scientific impulse, which is, in reality, neither *cogitare* nor *esse*, neither spirit nor matter, but rather that which for beings inhabiting the temporal realm is far more important than either: *life!*

Whether we elect to derive matter from spirit (or spirit from matter), or whether we should in the end seek to solve this relational conundrum by regarding both entities as aspects of some primordial system of polarities, as in the procedure adopted by our current proponents of the doctrine of "psycho-physical parallelism," all of these shifts will avail us nothing if, from the very outset, we have eliminated from our enquiries *the actuality of life*. Spirit *knows* and being *is*, but *only life can live!* Spirit and being dwell amidst generalities in a realm beyond time, whereas life participates in the temporal dimension that is also the realm of the individual. Without life, neither spirit nor matter could enable us to understand the nature of the temporal creation that is man. Now, however, we must avert our gaze from these somewhat academic disputes, in order that we may focus our attention more closely on the question as to the nature of consciousness.

Consciousness is not the stream of experience, for consciousness as such arises only when it has been stirred to activity by the lightning bolt of comprehension. We can derive definite empirical confirmation of this proposition from an examination of the forms in which life, even in its most miniscule incarnations, achieves phenomenal expression. We now come to the world of the plant. No age and no people has ever entertained the slightest doubt as to the propriety of attributing life to the plant, and indeed, both abstract thought and primitive speculation are as one in their inclination to see in the prolific and luxuriant primeval forest a far more suggestive image of the wealth of life than either abstract or primitive thought could perceive in the restless immobility that characterizes the animal kingdom. The prehistoric world's almost universal reverence for trees has its roots in this very soil. For all that, no one who has managed to liberate himself from the false notions that we have dismissed *supra*, will attribute consciousness to the plant, for he is now equipped with the gift of comprehension, regardless of whether he chooses to focus that gift upon the ray of sunlight, or upon the light of his own experience. We must now proceed to another vantage point, namely, that at which cognition and life enter into palpable association with each other.

The structural element of both plant and animal is the cell. Life persists solely through the operations of the cellular body. However, life as such is now and forever completely excluded from the dimension of consciousness. In every one of the innumerable births and deaths endured by transient organisms, the life of the cell persists without the slightest interruption all the way back to the protoplasmic entities that flourished in the primordial terrestrial seas. In spite of the fact that our conscious memory can recollect nothing whatever of our embryonic development within the womb, the living cell silently preserves the accumulated experience of our remotest ancestors. Since the life within us at any given moment is the transitory façade atop an incessantly driving flood, which, without pause or hindrance, rushes back to the geological epoch during which such crystalline formations as the schists were deposited, we can see that the duration of consciousness, in comparison with such temporal immensities, is precisely equivalent to the miniscule life-span of an individual person. Still, could it not be the case that life and consciousness are interchangeable entities?

We do not require a second glance outside to discover an instructive analogy, for consciousness resembles nothing so much as the sheet-lightning that over and over again flashes and flames above the waters of life, and which, from time to time, ignites a tight, white circle that blazes briefly. And whilst the lightning relinquishes the distant horizon unto a darkness utterly alien to consciousness, we are liberated at last from the tedium of the quotidian round. The alleged psychology of today condescendingly dismisses the whole area of "the prophetic gift," from presentiment, dream, and instinct, all the way to telepathy, clairvoyance, and visionary somnambulism (upon all of these things the Romantics speculated quite brilliantly; these thinkers grouped such phenomena under the comprehensive heading of the "nocturnal pole" of consciousness). Our contemporary psychologists are convinced that they reject all consideration of these matters in part because of their putative associations with the "occult," and in part because of certain alleged associations with half-baked medical theories. This attitude is not merely the expression of a philosophical hollowness; such blindness can only have had its origins in an exaggeratedly intellectualistic misapprehension of life. In the first place, insight clearly indicates that it belongs to the very nature of consciousness that it subsists in a sort of subjugation to rhythmical alternations such as those that transpire between kindled blaze and dimming flame, between seizing and releasing, and between waking and sleeping. Indeed, although the life of man rushes by in an uninterrupted continuity, it too is subject to the same law, for the life of a man is fated to be but a brief moment in the rhythmical alternation between birth and death.

On the other hand, we do have an intimate companion by our side for one-third of every day, for even consciousness experiences exhaustion, as it were, and must participate in our nightly slumbers; it is only then that we are aware neither of the ego nor of the world outside. No more conclusive evidence could be gathered to bolster our case on behalf of the radical difference of essence that characterizes consciousness and life, for whoever lumps the two together must logically conclude that the sleeper is, in fact, *dead*, until he is resurrected from death in the morning light. So untenable is the familiar notion that sleep and death are bound together as if by some strange affinity, that the healing, restorative, and constitutional powers of life are never more effectively enhanced than when we resort to the simple remedy of *deep sleep*! This truth is clearly communicated in the images that have come down to us from the legendary lore of Antiquity, for there we see characters drawn out of the dreams that came to them in the cavern of the Earth-mother, or in the temple of Asklepios, the sigils and premonitory visions of an *ecstatic* life as well as the regulations governing the procedures whereby the sickly could be restored to a *healthy* life. We all recognize these truths, even if many of us today seem to have forgotten their significance amidst the turmoil and banality of day-to-day considerations. Any man, no matter how consistently sober in demeanor he may appear to be, can certainly recall a moment during his youthful years when he awoke from slumber, feeling as if his soul had slyly slipped out of the protective maternal arms only to find itself exposed to the harsh glare of an inexorable light. He may well recall a mysterious emotion that grew within him, until he was overwhelmed by a feeling of homesickness on the part of the soul for its lost nocturnal life. The profound revelation that is communicated to us in the experience of such moods recalls the fairy tales (*Märchen*) that tell us of a lost paradise, and of those golden and silver ages during which, to employ an expression of Hesiod, men were like children or even like plants that sprout up from the soil. Afterwards, situated somewhat as Heracles was when confronted by the choice between life and spirit, mankind chose the road of thinking and willing, and, like Heracles, man has found naught upon that road but sorrow, hardship, and frightful adventures.

We have indicated that life and apprehension are incommensurable entities, and we have likewise grasped the distinguishing criteria of consciousness. Let us now extend the scope of our enquiry in order to determine what implications these discoveries entail for the nature of life, and what modifications might be incorporated in the natural sciences as well should it ever become feasible to replace the current mechanistic scheme with a doctrine of life. Bearing this purpose in mind, we now proceed to refute the familiar dogma that proclaims that life is merely a mechanistic process, and that the living body in particular may be accurately described as an intricate machine.

We attempted on one occasion to transport our self completely outside the sphere of active comprehension; we therefore chose the most simple, as well as the most basic procedure: perception. Now what can we grasp as being really true? Of course, someone might well venture to object that there could scarcely be a satisfactory answer to such a question. Nevertheless, it is only to the extent that something impinges upon our senses that we will be able to achieve an act of perception. Thus, there are innumerable things that are accessible to us: in space, which contains all that exists as if within a reservoir, the illimitable manifold of objects, such as stones, plants, animals, men, houses, countries, mountains, clouds, seas, constellations, and finally the similarly multiform movements of these and other things. It seemed to us at the time that this answer, although we had not foreseen its implications, in turn raised a problem, the solution to which seemed to us to promise very interesting results. Everything, in fact, that we have enumerated, along with everything that we could ever conceivably enumerate, can be described as a thing or object. We perceive things and the processes in which they become involved, such as rest and self-motility, arriving and departing, coming and going, in such a manner that we cannot even begin to grasp how we are able to perceive one object in yet another perspective.

For those who have already familiarized themselves somewhat with the relevant questions, we would like to introduce one more parenthetical observation at this point. Ever since the time of Locke, there have been discussions from time to time regarding something called "inner" perception; it is alleged that, more or less in the manner in which we deduce information from the actions of ghostly visitants, we receive knowledge of the world by piercing through the exterior aspect in order to comprehend the inner reality of perceived objects. We are in opposition to the viewpoint of the majority of contemporary psychologists who hold that it is not through perception, but through self-scrutiny that we gain our knowledge of man's inner life. If our psychologists could only prove the proposition in question conclusively, they would once more have reinforced their doctrine that the character of actuality inheres solely in *things*. However, is it not the case that this theory logically entails that its adherents ignore spaces, movements, and bodies and devote their time instead to investigating spirits and their acts of judgment, opinions, and volitions? The problem involved in this situation is identical to that involved in the case of the *thing*, in that spirits and their acts resemble things in that all of these entities "confront" us as fixed objects that somehow manage to remain unalterably the same even under the impress of the passage of time. So much for "inner" perception!

That which holds true for perceptive apprehension, likewise governs the process of apprehension in general; it links itself to objects and to nothing else. Therefore we must insist that, through mere apprehension, we can never obtain the slightest understanding of life. Were we to place ourselves before a spirit that is nothing but spirit, such as the god about whom the Christians inform us that he is omniscient, in that this god possesses the ability to predict the entire future, we should realize that this god is, in fact, subject to one significant limitation. Although this "spirit" sees and understands "all things," *he is and will remain completely ignorant of life*. Now, such a spirit would indeed be able to accurately gauge the positions of bodies as well as their internal processes; he would also be endowed with the ability to penetrate with his sharp eye into the very core of such physical structures as atoms and fluids, substances whose exhaustive analysis would require centuries of diligent labor on the part of our scientists; but even when that much has been conceded, this spirit could never participate in the stormy agitation at the heart of the living substance. The hither and thither mobility of creeping, running, and flying animals would be to him utterly indistinguishable from such phenomena as the fall of a stone, the moaning of the wind, and the turbulent movements of the waves upon the ocean. To such a spirit, the structural transformations undergone by a growing plant would appear to be identical in essence to the alterations that subtly alter the contours of a gradually eroding mountain peak. Both living and non-living entities reveal to him only the existential alterations in form that occur in mechanically driven things and molecules. To be sure, other spirits might appear before his penetrating gaze, spirits who are candid even in communicating their most cherished secrets and their as-yet unborn impulses. Nevertheless, he would never stake his all on any belief that such spirits were in any way intimately bound up with living, physical bodies. Outside of space and without location as they are, they are everywhere — *and nowhere*. The spiritual appears neither as a living expression of a bodily substrate, nor, conversely, does the bodily substance appear as the radius of action of the spiritual entity. The world thus collapses, falling into two completely alienated halves: a bodiless spiritual half and an embodied mechanistic half. All that we seem to lack, to paraphrase Goethe's poem, is "the living bond"!

The "divorce" to which we have just referred is not some idle fantasy, but rather a shabby rehash of a doctrine whose theoretical presentation was first formulated during Plato's lifetime. Nevertheless, the most flagrant and dogmatic revival of this style of thought began at the Renaissance. On one side, there is "matter"; on the other, we have "spirit." Now matter is spatial and embodied, while spirit is non-spatial and bodiless; matter obeys every law promulgated by our mechanistic science; spirit functions on the basis of an autonomous "freedom." We are confronted here by the self-same splitting of the world-image that we encountered earlier in our discussion of the Cartesian *cogitare* and *esse*, which we appropriated as our starting point on the road that has conducted us to our demonstration of the following truth: we can never formulate a concept of life if we insist on confusing life and concept. Let us now proceed by insisting that it belongs to the very nature of comprehension that it relates solely to the sphere of objects and mechanisms. Not only is thinking consciousness incapable of discovering life: it also possesses the ability to *murder* life. And whatever has been pierced by the searchlight of the intellect is instantaneously transformed into a mere *thing*, a quantifiable object for our thought that is henceforth only mechanically related to other objects. The paradoxical expression of a modern sage, "we perceive only that which is dead," is a lapidary formulation of a deep truth.

However, even if the terms "mechanistic" and "lifeless" should come to be regarded as interchangeable, we would still refuse to endorse the views of certain well-intentioned contemporary biologists who compound the reigning foolishness in their field by attempting to locate the definitive proof that the living body is not a machine in certain processes occurring in physical bodies. It *is* a machine, to the extent that we endeavor to comprehend its workings, just as it will remain perpetually *inconceivable* to the extent that it is alive. Those who announce that dead matter actually possesses the capacity to generate life are not simply committing an insignificant error of empirical observation, for theirs is an error whose sheer idiocy can in no way be regarded as inferior to that of the crackpot who has managed to convince himself that the meters, kilograms, and atomic weights with whose assistance we are able to quantify various natural processes, are in fact the very causative agents that bring about the manifold transformations in nature that they had been designed for the express purpose of measuring! Just as the longitudinal oscillation is certainly not the tone itself, but merely the quantifiable substratum underlying the tone, so too is the chemical-physical process transpiring in the living physical cell certainly not its life, but rather precisely that which is relevant to the condition, governed by strict enforcement of natural law, of its "material" (*dinglichen*) bearer. Does it not then appear to be the case that we must renounce our quest to formulate a science of life?

We must, in fact, abandon any such attempt so long as we remain stuck fast in the empty *cogitare*, since in lieu of this there is only the *esse*. No type of insight can be considered feasible under such circumstances other than that which can be rigidly fixed in "exact" concepts. An individual student may even relinquish every one of these options if that which is still referred to as "science" should, in the final analysis, seem in his eyes to be more like an initiation into some mystery cult; the only requirement in such a case is that he must not confuse his unpretentious thirst for knowledge with ignorance or uncertainty. When we summon up a recollection that affects us personally, the revived memory immeasurably enriches our living substance; indeed, we may be so compelled by the alluring charm of our recollected vision that we can only feel pity for the conventional scientist who must surely be tormented to distraction when he must attempt to satisfactorily account for the phenomenon! Life is not "observed," but it is *felt* with all of our darkest powers. And we are only able to achieve access to this feeling of living actuality with complete certainty in our deepest inwardness; beyond that, nothing can be definitely asserted. Whether we judge, assert, will or wish, dream, or fantasize, each and every one of these activities is supported and penetrated by the self-same stream of elementary emotional life, which is incomparable, irreducible, and beyond the reach of rationalization or coercion, for we are apodictically certain that life can never, ever be "grasped" (*begriffen*). And since we feel ourselves to be filled with this vitality, we therefore bring ourselves into that most intimate bond with the substance of life: the image of the world. Briefly put: we *experience* the personal and *participate in the experience of a stranger*. From that standpoint, it surely follows that we can know of life only that which our vitality allows us to know based solely on how deeply we are able to immerse our being in the vital substrate; a profound immersion in the substance of life will endow us with the ability to revive a living memory even within an enfeebled consciousness. It is not in the objectivity of outer and inner percepts, with their endless inventory of categories (of things, forces, causes, effects, and movements), but solely and utterly in an orientation toward the realm of experience, that we can establish an anchorage for the science of life. But now asymptotic formulae have banished the science of life from the living depths of the national spirit until at last, like a growing plant that vainly seeks for nourishment on a deforested continent, the national spirit is likewise stunted and deformed due to the relentless pressure of a leveling age.

We now must explore a world whose philosophy regards mechanistic, quantifying thought as having no independent existence whatsoever, and which regards the results achieved by such formalistic modes of thought as merely the conceptual precipitate that has been prescinded from a living entity. No living cell could ever have arisen upon the Earth if the Earth itself, as well as the entire universe, were not, in fact, a phenomenal manifestation of life. Likewise, the fall of the stone, the formation of the clouds, the torrential downpour of the rain, are outward expressions of life, and surely in the first rank of such expressions is the Earth, just as in the second rank we find the grander modes of interconnected cosmic life. The planetary systems, the firmament of the fixed stars, and the other astral phenomena richly proclaim the presence of a vital unity whose temporal duration so far exceeds the scope of human judgment that its very longevity makes it appear as if the cosmos receded from our gaze, leaving behind the impression of an ostensibly unchanging state, the characteristics of which are preserved in the crude expositions of our mechanistic empiricism. Every truly profound system of metaphysics must perforce valorize the primal actuality of life, just as every system of mathematics must valorize its own fundamental truths. The mechanical forces can be comprehended from the side of the living substance in the analytic process of mere understanding, but there is no reverse direction of apprehension by which an authentic comprehension of the substance of life can be derived from an analysis of mechanical forces. The core questions will remain: what sort of event transpired that enabled the planetary mode of life to culminate in cellular life; what potential transformations are still in store for life; what does the vital and eternally rhythmical pulse-pattern of "coming-to-be" and "passing away" mean to the planetary life; what is the meaning of death and life to the living organism; and how, finally, does the "macrocosm" effect changes within the "microcosm"?

In spite of all the chatter of yesterday and today on the topic of "progress," there have been prophetic souls who have drawn our attention to the implications of the indubitable increase of man's mastery (alas! along with man's destruction) of nature. But even these prophets have not devoted sufficient attention to the equally blatant assaults on the values of the soul; and some even attempt to introduce a certain balance into their meditations by insisting that, at the very least, our increased scientific knowledge will eventually enable us to recover our health and dispel the shadows that loom over our future. But it is only when we ignore the profound truth that man can indeed increase his store of knowledge without increasing his wisdom, and that he can likewise establish order without experiencing a concomitant yearning for beauty, that we feel compelled to oppose with all of our power the unthinking respect that has been accorded to modern science as well as to the course that it has set for itself. Contemporary science has, in effect, erected a hypertrophic "world-mechanism" (in the broadest sense of the word), which, we freely admit, no earlier age could ever have approximated. But science has also blinded itself to the point of hopelessness before the incomparably greater and more widely ramified question: *the question of life.* And surely the world has never before witnessed the spectacle of individuals who have become so wounded by their experience of the modern world that they would actively seek to establish connections with an earlier wisdom and with their ancestors, as if their greatest hope was that they might somehow successfully reverse the ominous course that the world has for so long seemed intent on pursuing! And indeed, from out of the vanished nineteenth century, and in spite of all of its technology and positivism, we must hail — for the creative work of these men of the last century has somehow survived the years, like splendid oases resisting the onslaught of the spreading wasteland known as "progress" — we must hail, I say, the dream-rich doctrine of life formulated by the German Romantics, as well as the mighty religion of life devised by Friedrich Nietzsche. Nevertheless, even though these participants in the Romantic movement had been favored with a far more rigorous training than any scholar had ever received before their time, and although they were additionally equipped with a far more sophisticated inventory of technical implements than any of their forerunners could ever have envisaged, those superb resurrections of past modes of life, which comprise the loftiest achievements of the Romantics, had long ago been completely surpassed by a similar group of inquisitive students, namely the pre-Socratics, those semi-mythical trailblazers of European thought, whose system of thought culminated in the so-called "hylozoism." The student who immerses himself, lovingly and wisely, in the symbolic language of the pre-Socratics must unfailingly conclude that no succeeding age—and especially not that of the pretentious twin peaks of Hellenic wisdom, Plato and Aristotle!—has matched, in sheer profundity and panoramic scope, those dazzling philosophical ruins that we continually visit in our quest for wisdom: Thales, Anaximander, Heraclitus, Empedocles, and Pythagoras are their names. The least that we say of these giants is that they were well on the way to the epochal discovery that an authentic interpretation of the world must entail a *doctrine of life*. They also understood full well that the *mechanistic* aspect of reality should be reduced to the status of an insignificant by-product of the living world. Precisely what experimental tools, methodological advances, and theoretical frameworks may be developed to assist researchers in devising a reformed doctrine of life, we are in no position to be able to predict. Perhaps it will be possible on some future occasion to delve more deeply into some of these matters, and to examine as well the treasure-trove of fresh ideas discovered by the great scientific visionaries who, even now, seek to establish the foundations of a more profound doctrine, a true science of life, which may ultimately render today's narrow-minded biological teaching obsolete.

CARL GUSTAV CARUS AS ROMANTIC THINKER (1930)

Ever since the author of these lines rediscovered the psychologist Carl Gustav Carus and was also able to demonstrate the profound relevance of his teachings for contemporary science, one does hear his name mentioned from time to time, but one must also ask: is anyone actually reading his works? It does seem, in fact, that in spite of the fact that many students now recognize his name, the true significance of his teaching goes unrecognized. Thus, before we can comprehend the intellectual situation in which Carus developed, we might mention some of the established facts in the story of his creative life.

Precisely four decades after the birth of Goethe, Carus was born in 1779 in Leipzig; his father was a master-dyer, and his mother was the descendant of a long line of brilliant natural scientists and medical men. His earliest conscious thought, he tells us in his *Denkwürdigkeiten* (Memoirs), occurred during the fifth year of his life, and his recollection is so characteristic of the man, that we now repeat it. In leafing through the pages of the old *Orbis pictus* of Amos Comenius, the boy stumbled upon an illustration bearing the inscription "The Human Soul." "There I saw the drawing of a table, upon which stood a triangle adorned with the eye of God and a sketch of a human figure." This chance event immediately caused him to turn his gaze to his inner world, and in a moment he was seized by the cryptic formula: "Even you possess a soul, even you are a soul," and for many days he was unable to get these words out of his mind; in fact, they were to haunt him down to the very day of his death.

In 1804, he attended the *Hochschule* in Leipzig, beginning his studies with botany, all the while sketching every plant species that he found in

the district; finally, he devoted himself passionately to anatomical studies, winning his doctorate in 1811 with *An Attempt at a General Theory
of Life*. In 1814, he became a full Professor and Director of the maternity
hospital in Dresden. He established gynecology as a discrete discipline,
worked on comparative anatomy (he provided his own illustrations for
his published work in this field!), and somehow managed to find sufficient time away from his medical practice to create brilliant oil paint-
ings depicting the seasons, landscapes, and architectural monuments in
which he took so much delight.

During this same period he became friendly with Caspar David
Friedrich; in 1818 he inaugurated his correspondence with Goethe,
whom he was to visit in Weimar on July 21, 1821. He traveled widely,
visiting such places as Rügen, Prague, Switzerland, and Genoa. His
studies, which were incredibly comprehensive in their scope, dealt not
only with the biology of living organisms, but extended as well into such
fields as geology, paleontology, cranioscopy, physiognomics, "vital magnetism," landscape painting, epistemology, metaphysics, and research
into the history of literature. His final tally of published works soars to
81, but that number does not tell the whole story of his productivity, for
most of his works appeared in multi-volume sets!

In 1827 Carus was appointed to the prestigious position of personal
physician to the king of Saxony, and he was to remain at that post until
his death in 1869.

There can be no doubt that Carus was one of the greatest scientists to
emerge from the period to which historians have given the unfortunate
name of "Late Romantic." The so-called "late" Romantics were, in fact,
the consummate Romantics, for the "early" Romantics did not fully
deserve the name. Even now the name "Romantic" has led to numerous misunderstandings, which suggest comparisons with the pseudo-
distinctions that have been alleged to exist between a "Roman" and a
"Foreign" spiritual tendency. Likewise, one must occasionally endure the
parsonic prattle of the enemies of the Romantics, who insist that the
Romantic movement was merely a stopover on the reactionary high-
road to a full-fledged revival of "Catholicism" (ignoring the fact that the
charge holds true only for a mere handful of the movement's adherents).
The heart of the matter is that the Romantics' greatest achievement was
in developing a completely unprecedented vision of the world of actuality.

Likewise, the Romantics represented a completely Germanic mode of contemplation. No non-German land can seriously entertain the claim of precedence for one of their own candidates, for no non-German writer ever approached the lofty achievements of the great German Romantics.

The German Romantics formed a unified front against the mindless cult of "reason" that so agitated eighteenth century Europe, in large part because, unlike their rivals, the Romantics were never animated by the obsessive classicism of the Hellenic revival, preferring instead to examine their own German past; and in this process the Romantics rediscovered, and reaffirmed, the greatness of the Gothic Middle Ages just as they opened up a whole new field of study in their research into the cultural genius of the prehistoric Germanic world. And the Romantics were not merely a band of wandering poets and dreamers, for they also created a Romantic music and a Romantic style in painting, a uniquely Romantic style of historiography, a Romantic ethnology, and even a Romantic doctrine of political economy! Transcending all these achievements was their creation of an idiosyncratically Romantic school of natural science. In every one of the fields that we have mentioned, the German Romantics became the truly significant pathfinders. Names like Niebuhr, Schlosser, Raumer, Ranke, Arndt, Jakob and Wilhelm Grimm, are just a few among the countless creators of that imperishable intellectual revolution known as Romanticism, and they have provided us with a rich legacy that even now is making brilliant contributions to cultural history.

And the same holds true in the scientific fields. The very first formulation of the cellular theory, in fact, was the work of Lorenz Oken. The theory of evolutionary development, which arranges all organic life into a series of transformations, has its source in the speculations of the Romantic "Nature-Philosophers." Cuvier, Goethe, Geoffrey, and Treviranus were the forerunners, von Baer and—above all—Carus, were the most powerful preservers and extenders of this tradition of evolutionary theory, which has, of course, ruled the scientific universe ever since. Finally, let us dismiss the blatantly mendacious *fable convenue* whispered by those fools and faddists who insinuate that the Romantics never made a genuine discovery that was not preordained by a very partisan oracle, namely, their "wish-fantasies." The Romantics justly preferred to regard them as inner convictions!

The Romantics knew full well that they had involved themselves in a bitter war of the spirit that was already raging ceaselessly and savagely between the vital worldview of the Romantics and the dictatorship of the

Enlightenment saviors, who preached that perpended world-as-machine "philosophy" that these shamans of the mechanistic apocalypse insisted would be man's salvation.

Sadly, the mechanistic apostles had already triumphed in one campaign after another from the middle of the previous century and down to the age of Carus, but it is only fair to recognize that the mechanistic movement's publicists and prophets were themselves probably unaware of the sinister fact that their banal theories were being remorselessly exploited in order to enrich and empower one particular social class, specifically, the cash-crazed technocrats who were mounting the Industrial Revolution even as the Romantics waged their quixotic war against the machine-worship that was soon to enslave even the machine's victims.

Admittedly, the Romantics had their own limitations (one of the few things that they possessed in common with the rest of "mankind"). They were also bogged down in the Platonic worship of "ideas," a crippling error that they compounded by incorporating the equally disastrous notion — probably influenced by Goethe's adoption of the same idea — that behind the unconscious processes that transpire within the living world, there exists a type of "World-Reason" that keeps everything in line. Nevertheless, their errors have perished for the most part, or at least the influence that their false doctrines once exerted has been diminished appreciably, and nothing can ever change the fact that it is to the German Romantics that we owe the imperishable treasures that they discovered within their own visionary hearts.

When we ask ourselves what was the source of that unique vision of the Romantics, the clear and unambiguous answer resounds: the Romantic thinkers sought to follow Goethe's example by focusing their attention less upon the *causes* that brought about the phenomena before them, and more upon their *meaning*. However, they also recognized — and in this area, in fact, they went far beyond the scope of Goethe's research — that the universe can only be comprehended as a realm in which phenomenal essences — *souls* — appear. As a result their natural science entailed an attendant psychology, just as their psychology entailed a comprehensive system of natural science. No Romantic had a clearer perception than Carus of the way in which science and art led to a unified existence at the deepest level of life, and this insistence upon the innermost indivisibility of science and art became a slogan that he employed on numerous occasions as a true description of his intellectual mission. Just as Carus sought to indicate the visible signatures that identify specific forms of planetary life in his landscape painting, so also did he employ the methods of natural science in order to inscribe the nature of that planetary life in the appropriate scientific formulae.

The richest fruit to emerge from these meditations was his treatise *Psyche: On the Developmental History of the Soul.* The first edition of this treatise, which he had begun to work on during 1843, was brought out by the publisher Michaelis in 1846. The second edition appeared in 1851 (Diederichs has recently brought out a reprint of this second edition).

Carus was well aware of the outstanding value of this work, which in later years he would always describe as the closest to his heart of all his published treatises.

Let us now present a brief sketch of at least the main points proclaimed in this treatise. If it is true that the soul is identical with that which the ancients called the "principal of life" (an idea, of course, that has been forgotten since the age of Descartes), then it must be the case that the soul cannot be divided into component parts any more than it can have received its nature from the addition of discrete components that can be assembled to form a whole. Since Descartes, however, a completely erroneous doctrine has infected the science of psychology due to the reigning superstition that psychology can only achieve results by basing itself upon a program of mathematical quantification—and this is something that has long been the established practice among researchers of the "mechanistic" persuasion, a school that prospers today beyond its dreams. Carus holds that just as the organism is formed from the fertilized cell from which developmental phase it begins to differentiate itself, thus every transformation of the soul is a process of development, and as such it has no conceivable resemblance to the mere collection of measurable points or to the process whereby a factory worker assembles a machine out of its discrete components.

If the soul is the principle of life, then we are justified in concluding that it cannot also be synonymous with *consciousness.* Every cell that makes up our body lives, but its life and experience is as devoid of the faculty of consciousness as a house plant. When we observe life in its antithetic relationship to consciousness, we discover something that Goethe was the first to comprehend and to which he gave the name "unconscious," which is the reason why Carus explicitly states on the very first page of *Psyche* that "the key to an understanding of conscious thought resides in the realm of the unconscious." Any thinker who sought to exhaust the implications of that proposition would soon discover that a human lifetime is not sufficient to permit him to achieve his goal. We will restrict ourselves here to drawing your attention to just three points.

Since the age of Descartes, philosophers have directed their attention to the nature of moods, feelings, rages, and so on; and yet after all the time they have devoted to these matters, they find themselves precisely where the founders of the rationalist school of thought began: thus, feelings are *perturbationes animi*, or — to put it more cautiously — they are dark, chaotic thoughts. One may recall in this connection the elevation of feeling that occurs when we witness a sunset or when we listen to a Beethoven symphony. Nevertheless, there are defective doctrines at work here, all of which must be overturned before we can arrive at a purely philosophical analysis of these discoveries. It is at this precise point that one may first be struck by the intuitive conviction that the "cult of reason" and the cult of nihilism are thick as thieves with each other.

However, since the age of Carus, we are able to understand that feelings — and this holds true of every conceivable species — merge their substance with consciousness from moment to moment under the governance of the overall condition of the body, which in turn experiences transformations under the influence of the impressions that fall upon the senses. The inherently unconscious processes of life exert their influence upon consciousness, and the resultant effects we call feelings, and this fact satisfactorily accounts for the obvious ability of an access to joy to improve the condition of the organism, just as an increase in sorrow or melancholy limits and diminishes the organism. Why, for instance, do intoxicating beverages produce their familiar effects? Carus understands why, and he explains that the chemical processes involved link the living organism to the condition of the soul that results from the consumption of alcohol. Therefore, there does indeed exist a "spirit of wine"!

Further, all living processes occur rhythmically; one recalls the pulses, the respiration, the alternation between sleep and waking. In addition, we must understand that every consciousness necessarily sinks periodically into the unconscious, and it is at those times that the healing processes transpire.

There can never be an identical repeat of a so-called representation. It is much more accurate to say that a representation will either fade and disappear or it will elevate itself and thereby acquire a "nimbus." One may recall the joyous blossoming of one's youth, which remains in memory long after childhood has ended. Our consciousness bears the colors of our own nature, and our character reaches into our most sublime meditations.

Finally, the loss of awareness that accompanies a profound and dreamless sleep is not to be interpreted as a decrease in life, for in the most acute sense it represents a growth and an improvement in the vital powers. Meanwhile, the limits that divide the conscious life from the unconscious may collapse, resulting in the possibility that those limits which separate the organism from the life of the world will also disappear. It was in the pondering of thoughts such as these that the Romantics were led to investigate the phenomena of somnambulism, dreams, clairvoyance, presentiments, and also to discover whether or not an infection of the soul could be alleviated by the application of the healing powers of magic. Still, Carus would not have been the grand Apollo of the spirit that he always remained if he did not carefully protect his mind from the influence of certain incautious exaggerations to which such meditations might lead.

Nevertheless, even in his most Platonic moments, Carl Gustav von Carus stands out as one of the greatest, as well as one of the last, of the authentic Romantic thinkers.

ON THE VALUE OF SCIENCE (1930)

Before we can hope to answer the question concerning the real value of science, one would be well advised to prepare oneself, paradoxically, by asking another, more basic question; namely, what does one mean, precisely, by the word "science"? One must also evaluate with some judiciousness the nature and worth of those other extant values with which science competes for preeminence in our lives. When we overhear some naïve soul hold forth with such canting nonsense as "science has already decided…" and so forth, we must beware that we ourselves do not succumb to the false notion that science, as the highest of all values, is uniquely endowed with the capacity to generate categorically valid judgments. One can hardly conceive a more hollow proposition. On the other hand, of course, there have always been those truths that have managed to gain first the interest of, and ultimate vindication from, the scientific establishment only decades or even centuries after they were discovered. The more apodictically certain the scientist is as to the ultimate validity of the procedure whereby he has alighted upon his experimental findings, the less valid will his deliberations turn out to have been, in the final analysis. To an even greater extent, it is the experimental demonstration, or that which gives at least the appearance of being such, that makes of these researches something that most scientists feel fully justified in describing as true science; and the facts are, again, validated for these students when they have properly conducted the experiment in question. They seek some measure of experimental certitude through the utilization of the methodology of quantitative formalism, which, they insist, can provide a solid guarantee of valid results only if the researcher has ignored the influence of personal affects, or emotional stressors, in order to attend to the precise measurement of the quantities that constitute the sole aim of all experimental research. Bearing this

106

notion in mind, the scientist must conform his behavior to the dictates of a code that values nothing in the world more highly than "factuality," for it is this very attention to "factuality" on the part of the researcher that serves as the sole guarantor of the validity of his experimental work. Finally, we are more than willing to admit that every conceivable species of philosophical "irrationalism" currently on the market, whether the "irrationalist" seeks to substitute this brainstorm or that flash of inspiration, or some other stray burst of intuitive "insight," necessarily possesses no more inherent truth content than a mere desert mirage or feverish hallucination.

Bearing these observations in mind, let us recognize also that the will-to-objectivity must never be erroneously promoted to the post of automatic guarantor that the student who possesses this invaluable volition will enjoy a successful outcome in every bit of research to which he devotes his time. For one thing, erroneous notions will persistently tempt the student to ignore certain inconvenient realities. One especially troublesome fact that often escapes the attention of the novice is that behind the *conscious* purposes that he assures himself are animating his mind even when confronting the most intractable difficulties (examples of which, of course, will block the path to truth for every researcher at one time or another), other purposes — the "driving forces," to speak the language of characterology — a man's personal "interests," are oftentimes at work in the subterranean depths of the unconscious, from which emerge the honey-sweet and gently whispered invitations to false philosophy posted by those unconfessed and scarcely recognized messages transmitted by the "driving forces." Such lures have clouded the will-to-objectivity and thereby compromised the intellectual probity of scientific investigators throughout Western history (one is compelled, paradoxically, to inscribe upon the list of these beguiled and self-deceived sages even one or two who even now occupy — and deservedly so — the very pinnacles of scientific fame). However, the quite savage criticisms that, even as we speak, are being launched against the sciences from every conceivable direction, turn out upon closer scrutiny to be aimed not against science in general, but only against the particularly tendentious and ill-considered manner in which science has developed in the post-Renaissance period. The direction that we are pondering has flourished so richly that it has at last become the one and only method that is regarded as universally valid. The inner meaning of this trend was perceived quite early on in the timeframe in question; thus, we find a thinker like Auguste Comte distilling the central doctrine until it has been reduced to his formulaic slogan: *voir pour prévoir*. It was only what was to be expected that since Comte's time, the orthodox scientist explicitly assures us that he sees his mission to be the ultimate enslavement of nature to the demands of man's will. It has not escaped the notice of alert students, however, that there is the very species of science that seeks to discover the laws that regulate nature; specifically, the analysis of physical forces and chains of causality whose solution is determined through the statistical analysis of the relevant data. The sole imperative governing this approach is the compulsion to quantify the whole natural world in order to constrain its processes under the governance of the will-to-cognition.

On the other hand, there exists a radically different perspective on cognition whose earliest, as well as loftiest, manifestation transpired during the golden age of Greek philosophy, and this achievement exerted a profound influence upon Medieval scholasticism, although speculative metaphysicians during the Middle Ages were constrained by the crippling influence of the regnant church authorities, who coerced thinkers into strict conformity with the superstitions and dogmas of their cult. Man seeks to develop knowledge as to the nature of the world, and he also endeavors to comprehend the forces that function as the foundations of that world; likewise, he is compelled to delve into questions as to the origins of that world, which desires an answer to the question as to whether the workings of the world-process have been pre-determined under the constraints of a strict teleology that pursues, in some as yet undetermined manner, an ultimate goal whose attainment has been decreed by destiny, or, on the contrary, whether the world-process had no beginning just as it will have no end, and whose heartbeats pulsate in a rhythmic pattern that alternates between the coming-to-be and the passing-away of cosmic processes and telluric life-forms, a process that is analogous to the ceaseless, rhythmic swinging to-and-fro of the pendulum in a clock. Above all, when the initial question as to the primary object sought by the researcher is broached, we find that the experimental scientist, who brags insistently about his wide-open gaze on the real world, suddenly announces that his empire now embraces every conceivable formulation of distinctions which, we are stunned to be informed, must always remain beyond the sphere of man's non-experimentally-derived competence! How clearly this insight reveals the strange fear that obsesses materialistic scientists, namely, the haunting dread that every estimation of value and quantitative sanity will be shattered to a million fragments at the very instant when we admit the possibility that man may actually possess an intellectual faculty that enables him to make genuine discoveries of a metaphysical nature! The discoveries that have been achieved by scientists who espouse a methodological formalism based upon an alleged universally applicable quantifiability of everything that exists, are no more significant to the goals of genuine science than so many additional tools at a work-site. And it is precisely these "exact" findings that in truth provide the student with nothing more earth-shaking than an advanced yard-stick that should increase somewhat our extant store of cognitive data. On top of that, this whole formalistic methodology has never, and CAN never, succeed in any one of its attempts to engage in research into the mysteries of human consciousness.

If the student should be unable or unwilling in any significant measure to comprehend the broadly sketched outlines that we have drawn thus far, he will thereby have prevented his understanding from gaining access to a significant dimension of insight into our exposition of the matter at hand. It is important that we all bear in mind that, to the extent that any student involves his thinking brain in scientific research, he has thereby embarked upon a course of activity that he must regard as entailing his trafficking with a *substantial reality*, namely "actuality" (*Wirklichkeit*). From our historical studies, however, we know that it was comparatively late in the evolution of human development, such as in ancient Greece, or, more precisely, with the advent of Protagoras, that we find individual thinkers undertaking the first truly rigorous attempt to demonstrate successfully, by means of strictly logical procedures, that science could lay just and incontrovertible claims to possess firm foundation in truth's bedrock. Shortly after that epochal event, and building directly upon that very achievement, the Greek philosophers worked out a unique and unprecedented mode of research, namely epistemology (*Erkenntnislehre*), or, to put it more precisely still, "the science of cognition" (*Bewusstseinswissenschaft*), that modality of reasoning or meditating upon processes or actions that examines psychical processes and spiritual acts as elements transpiring within the structured cosmos that houses man and enables him to conduct social action; now science would for the first time be able to shed some light on political man as well as natural processes. From these investigations, in the fullness of time, there developed even more astonishing branches of epistemological research, among which we may mention the "theory of perception"

(*Wahrnehmungslehre*). If we seek for an example of the influence exerted by these epistemological advances upon the development of recent science, we have no need to look any further than the field of modern physics (taking the designation "physics" in the broadest sense of the word).

We have previously expressed certain reservations regarding what seem to us to be untenable and even counterproductive approaches to the larger problems involved in the striving for cognitive certitude. Not an insignificant number of scientists have recently responded to the perceived impasse with the novel claim that "actuality," as well as such "truths" that we can pronounce regarding the nature of that actuality, can best be validated on the basis of whatever "works" for us at the time ("pragmatism," they call it). Many proponents of this "philosophy" occupy their time with physics, since it is the most cherished conviction of this school that their beloved experimental work, when conducted in the modern laboratory under the most stringent system of controls and safeguards, forms the soundest foundation for any valid research program, while also furnishing the student with a guarantee that he is doing science in the strict sense of the word. Thus, armed with this experimental *sine qua non*, he is perfectly prepared to test the truth content (or lack of such) embodied in a particular hypothesis, and to determine whether or not the suggested hypothesis turns out to be a mare's nest of flummery or a brilliantly constructed theory that should enable us to discover previously unknown truths. The philosopher of the pragmatic school derives additional satisfaction from the seemingly universal inability of rival scholars, who seem utterly incapable of mounting a credible critique of the claims by pragmatists that they have, finally and permanently, banished all "wish-fantasies" from laboratory work and from the refereed journals in which that lab work is preserved, like flies in amber, so that it may be rendered forever beyond reproach or cavil. To this conviction we must respond by insisting that the question as to the nature of actuality is indeed a metaphysical conundrum; the physical scientists have thus far sought to evade our attempts to acquire certain necessary clarifications from their hands regarding these matters, and they have resorted to the completely illegitimate importation of an obviously false doctrine into the debate, namely, their utterly wretched attempt to portray the living cosmos and man himself as if they were mere machines and no more than clanking mechanisms. When we scrutinize such highly ingenious experimental research, what we really discover is nothing but thousands of cases and countless instances of "potentialities," every one of which can be formulated as follows: if you perform such and such operations upon the physical force or substance in question, you will inevitably encounter such and such results. But consider for a moment: would we not explode with laughter at the housewife who wanted to define water — without which, admittedly, she could not produce her cakes — as "cooked liquidity"! But we indulge in a similar species of idiocy when we seek to reduce actuality to the status of a mere by-product, or epiphenomenal residue deposited by man's manufacturing processes, an error that obviously results from the effects wrought by the very governing bias that helped to design the experimental operation in the first place!

We have already alluded to the belief that is so widely entertained by contemporaries that we now stand upon the loftiest peak ever reached by science, although we must qualify that notion by restricting that model of science to the somewhat constricted arena wherein pure cognition and quantitative formalism is monarch of all he surveys. We would be more than justified this once, I am sure, if we were to tap into our small reserves of cynicism at this juncture, however, for we all know that certain very earthly interests may play more than an insignificant part in conducting hostile interventions, to put it politely, into the researcher's laborious campaign to discover authentic truths. Nevertheless, this insight has been resolutely ignored by the architects of every philosophical system of an idealistic cast since the days of Plato, who ascribed reality solely to his "Ideas," as well as by every builder of mechanistic, or materialist, systems since the time of Democritus, who sponsored his own candidate, specifically "atoms," for the office of most "real" being (subsequent office holders have been "ions," "electrons," and so on, until today we are treated to the ghostly doings of the illustrious "quanta," which feature so prominently in current lectures on "quantum mechanics"). Now we wish to suggest, and we will be excused, hopefully, if we raise this concern with some vehemence at this juncture, that the proposition that we are about to adduce expresses no more than the absolute truth of the matter in hand: and with the aid provided by our access to the insight provided by this simple truth, we identify the agency whose operations result in every conceivable species of epistemological error as spirit (*Geist*). Every conceivable scientific interest that encourages us to consider "being" and "actuality" as perfect synonyms causes us, to the precise measure that our wishes are permitted to hobble our love for the truth, to decorate the self-mastery of the human spirit with the beautiful plumes that should actually adorn world-creative genius. The object of the idealist thinker's cognitive strivings possesses no "actuality" content; in fact, the mill can of course grind corn into cornmeal, if we may employ an analogy, but the situation of the student of the "object" is a dismal one, for his "object" is no more than an unconscious product of the mill—the grinding, destructive mill—of understanding! But what value has this sort of speculation that alone deserves to be designated as the independent will-to-cognition? Indeed, one might even venture to inquire whether this rare mode of scientific apprehension ever existed on Earth in the first place!

This style of apprehension has indeed appeared at several junctures in the history of the West over the past three and one-half millennia, just as it has achieved great prominence in the Far East, and, in fact, it has not yet completely perished from the Earth even now. It is unfortunately not feasible for me to provide even the sketchiest historical outline of the lives and doctrines of the members of this select group on this occasion. Nevertheless, I will make brief mention of a particular scientist, whose genius was such that his career, even when scanned *in nuce*, as it were, provides more than sufficient matter for our expository purposes. The man to whom I allude was, of course, the great German polymath Johann Wolfgang von Goethe. He was a poet, an artist, and a sage, among many other outsize accomplishments, although he was certainly not someone whom we could be comfortable in characterizing as a philosopher or even as a comprehensively trained scientist—in the technical sense of those terms, that is. In spite of these facts, it was Goethe alone who was able to envision the prophetic path upon which he would receive that inspired, and inspiring, ability that enabled him to distill the vital essence of the phenomenological approach to the study of nature, and to formulate the first draft of a biocentric worldview, regardless of his own admitted lack of a thorough grounding in the bare facts of the disciplines that he was, nonetheless, to enlarge and enrich with his wisdom and vision as no other contemporary could have done. Therefore, let us choose one of Goethe's statements that seems to express, with a finished flair, the type of science to which he was to devote so many of his later years: "Those who seek for truth behind the phenomena are condemned to an expedition in search of nothingness—the phenomena themselves are the living truth!" On other occasions, he speaks in a similar vein of the "primordial phenomenon" and a "visionary power of judgment."

We would be wise to remain attuned at all times to detect the return from obscurity of a species of thought that from time to time seems to resurface, although the revivals of this "science of the appearances" ("phenomenology"—in our own strict sense) have been, for the most part, short-lived and fragile. The biocentric version of phenomenology holds that the images themselves are the reality, and that there is no other vague entity lurking behind the images in order to substantiate their claims as *realia*—not atoms, not quanta, not ideas, not spirit, and not the laws of spirit. With this in mind, we should proceed to the next stage of our meditations, which takes us to the point at which we are able to comprehend the transitory nature of actuality; if nothing "real" stands behind or beneath "reality," as its ontological or transcendental guarantor, then there can be no unchanging substance perduring within phenomena throughout all of their existential transactions and permutations. Now Goethe was the archetypal man of the eye, a visually- and spatially-oriented person without a peer; but there were others, who had diverse styles of vision, among whom we may mention the late Romantic thinkers, and, somewhat later still, Friedrich Nietzsche, all of whom can be more accurately characterized as quintessential men of cosmic rhythms, those seers whose bodies and souls lived in such profound intimacy with rhythmic alternations that their inner worlds were linked with the pulsations of the cosmos surrounding them. We must follow these earlier visionaries and incorporate their ruling principle as our guide that the sole verities are, in fact, the images and their actuality, for only with this principle held firmly in mind will we be able to overturn the ever-mounting assault of the appropriative-purposive mode of thought that has grown into a veritable monster, in spite of all that so many obfuscators have done during so many centuries to blind themselves and their pupils to this rock-solid truth. I need not remind the learned reader that no previous methodological reform that has been suggested in this area has ever managed to bear wholesome fruit; as a matter of fact, every previous candidate has unfailingly managed to land its champions in a hopelessly tangled web of contradictory propositions and dogmatic quandaries. Of course, we are willing to make an exception for logic, which has, we admit, made some genuine strides in recent decades, although we feel that none of our philosophers should be indulging in premature orgies of self-congratulation at this point in time (the student who wishes to probe more deeply into the issues involved here should consult the relevant technical treatises published by the author of these lines), since it is painfully clear already that the path on which philosophy has already set its foot is encumbered by dangerous obstacles that may turn out to be either useless timewasters in the best-case scenarios, or—in the worst—may well be wonderfully inviting vistas that lure the student ever further down lost highways from which he will never return.

We have already glanced at the "pure" form of the will-to-cognition in comparison with the other, radically distinct, scientific methodology, and our conclusion must be that these two species are, in fact, directing their energies toward two utterly discrete realms of actuality, a realization that, in turn, provides us with more than a mere hint that the one variety inhabits an intellectual domain that is incommensurable with the other. We have indicated which of the two paths is passable and which presents certain difficulties. One can, however, when confronted with pointed objections to the "uselessness" of genuine knowledge, respond by framing one's own questions: why on Earth does man wish to acquire wisdom of the genuine sort if the very quest for such knowledge does not, and indeed cannot, in fact, provide him with what he feels to be a significant release from inner distress? And: might there not exist somewhere else another set of conditions to which we may somehow gain access; and further that, in that place, those very conditions might permit man to live out a much more complete or fulfilled mode of life than the caricature of life that he seems to have been thus far condemned to serve out as if he were some hardened criminal, by a criminal court whose judge decided upon sentences that were predetermined by the punitive demands of the will to cognition!

At this juncture, however, one must acknowledge the fact that our disputants are no longer seeking a solution to one rather narrowly delimited query as to the value of science. Rather they are beginning to question the very value of thinking consciousness itself, and that question, of course, opens up for investigation a far vaster region of the sciences of the spirit (*Geisteswissenschaften*) to the more analytical and curious natures among us. The particular response that each student will provide to the far more comprehensive query that we are alluding to here is *not* merely a matter of individuals and their tastes, to be the subject matter of a multiple-choice survey listing fool-fodder questions, the answers to which are determined by consulting vague whims and transient fancies, and then professionally vetted and "corrected" before publication in the daily rag.

On the contrary, we must realize that, in the end, we are here dealing rather with science, with spirit, and—with the darker voices and stranger stirrings that have their deepest springs *in the power of our will*. Therefore, the organism, although it is entitled by all means to its moments of rapture, must also be prepared to ask (and to answer!), among all the other persistent questions that confront it, such a simple query as how this individual is to live and breathe among so many other living beings! For it is certainly the case that in primordial epochs man was not quite the intellectual giant that he believes himself—and with justice!—to be today; and we must also realize that at some subsequent epoch in ("geological") time, man will undoubtedly lose some significant portion of the power of that renowned brain-box of which he is so proud once again. In any case, although his past, primordial state or his ultimate future condition might seem, at first blush to imagination's hazy gaze, as a more fulfilling state of being than does our own awkward betwixt-and-between status, we can be sure that, were we to experience life at such a (shall we say?) compromised *niveau*, we would certainly judge the experience to have been—at least as we are so constituted at this moment—as an almost inconceivably, unutterably impoverished one. So—let us at least share the hope that such an eventuality may not arrive prematurely, agreed?

Nature vs. Nurture (1935)

I wish to say a word or two on the omnipresent and indeed vexing question as to whether a child's character is already formed at birth ("genetically pre-determined") or whether it is environmentally conditioned (fully "plastic," as in the *tabula rasa* (blank slate) in the strict style of English empirical thought); the woods are also home, as one might expect, to half-hearted and more tepid variants of these two which might be taken into consideration, and so we acknowledge the existence of those researchers who hold that the human personality is a little bit of this, but, refreshingly, also a little bit of that (partially gene-determined, but also partially "plastic," in other words, subject to considerable environmental conditioning). Having noted their existence, we move on.

Therefore, for the most part, we shall find one educator saying, "The character of this child is inborn and unalterable"; and he will be quite correct. Likewise, another educator will assure us that: "This student's personality is the resultant of the numerous societal and familial pressures and influences that have been brought to bear upon him during his childhood years"; he too will be correct!

We intend to tease you with no cheap paradox in endorsing both of these views; rather, we are merely seeking to draw attention to the fact that the rival authorities are in fact employing the substantive "character" in two distinct denotative, or "lexical," senses. So let us clarify, as best we may, these contentious meanings, and let us see if we can do this without wandering from our psychological reservation.

We do all agree, I take it, that the character not only of man, but of every living organism upon our planet, is genetically endowed; but there are also, I believe we should also agree, other types of earthly formations whose structural integrity is an unalterable quality of their very being, as for example the molecular architecture of "rock crystal," which we feel justified in describing as "pre-determined." But the situation is very different indeed with the most highly organized form of terrestrial organism, namely the human being, since every person carries around with him, as if he were equipped with a virtual playing-field of evolutionary possibilities, whose precise dimensions and contours he has yet to determine. Just as surely as a man grows older with every minute that passes, and just as surely as an aged body is no longer that of a child, so surely is it that the nature of an aged man is not that of a young child. But what is it precisely that remains unaltered throughout all the changes that the body has endured as it passes through the changes from youth to old age? This is only one of those questions the answers to which will be found only after we have developed our finest powers of discrimination and our richest powers of observation in learning just how the characterologist formulates accurate judgments in his field.

One crucially important consideration must be born in mind by the student: every researcher and every educator who has been entrusted with the mission to teach the young must be strictly prevented, by the full force of the law, from illicitly gleaning information about his young charges from documents on file when his sacred trust is to be educating them in the classroom — in person.

A genuinely responsible educator devotes his life to the minds and souls of his pupils; he determines the nature of their dispositions and he estimates their adaptabilities; but — again, I must emphasize this point — he must never permit himself or anyone on his staff to employ a sneak-thief's access to a file-folder in such a way as to prejudice a student's future, such as by rumor-mongering about "degeneracy," or by making cheap shots about "flawed character structure" rooted in "unfortunate ancestry" or "violent upbringing." When a young student has come this far in his schooling, the chief question that should concern the educator is no longer whether nature or nurture rules the roost — not even the most blasé academic could feign an interest in the praxis here — all that we demand now is that the educator attempt to assist his student as he tries to achieve such results as are within his reach!

The Problems of
Psychology (1952)

I n pondering the "problems of psychology," I will refrain from speaking of the "soul" according to the usages of those persons who have
floated a doctrine of psychology whose sole connection with a genuine
science of the soul is a matter of mere semantics. These psychologists
ordinarily while away their hours investigating the connections that exist between sensory experience and neurological processes, or else they
ponder thinking, feeling, and willing, which are quite discrete processes,
although our "psychologists" seldom seem to be able to grasp this fact.

A more authentic concept of the soul has existed since the dawn of
Western thought, the ramifications of which are founded upon the hypothesis that man's nature comprises a three-fold, or "triadic," structure
whose components are: body—soul—spirit. This doctrine constitutes
one of the loftiest achievements of philosophical speculation among
the ancient Greeks, and no subsequent thinker who has endeavored
to evade the vital truth embodied in this idea of the "three-fold" has
met with the slightest success in his philosophizing. In fact, the three-
fold has been a constant theme throughout the history of philosophy,
at times becoming buried beneath obscure formulae, but nevertheless
enduring in one avatar or another from the ancient Greeks, through
the Middle Ages, and even beyond that tragic and blind age that convinced itself—as well as posterity—that such metaphysical niceties
had, with one fell blow, been rendered obsolete upon the discovery
of the philosophical system elaborated by the French mathematician
and philosopher Descartes, whose predilection for dualistic schemes
encouraged him to devise a doctrine that presented the world and man

himself as divided between a *bodily*, or spatial half, and a *spiritual*, or thinking half.

There have been several significant campaigns mounted in the post-Cartesian epoch, whose proponents labored to revive a theoretical analogy to the tripartition scheme advanced by the Greek philosophers. For instance, an unconscious attempt to bridge the gap between ancient Greek speculations and modern thought was undertaken by Goethe himself during the course of his investigations in the field of biology, and these studies were subsequently developed, refined, and systematized by the philosophers of the German Romantic movement.

In the afterglow of the Romantic noontide, however, the soul either disappeared completely from the precincts of psychological research, or it was grotesquely confused with some other entity whose true nature was utterly alien to that of the soul. I believe that I can justly claim, on the basis of the relevant research that I have conducted over several decades, that I have been able to establish the reality of this "three-fold" or triadic division of man's being upon a rigorous scientific foundation, and I believe also that I have achieved my results with such interpretative exactitude that we can now determine with great precision what proportion of our nature stems predominantly from the soul, what proportion from the body, and what proportion, finally, stems from the spirit.

Wherever we go today, we hear a lot of empty babbling about primordial mankind (*Urmenschen*), in spite of the fact that no one has ever encountered such a being. There have indeed been pre-historical tribes (*aussergeschichtliche Völker*), falsely called "primitives," such as the pre-historical people to whom the Greeks gave the name Pelasgians, whose reign was ended by the great flood that preceded the advent of Deukalion and Pyrrha, and whose descendants became known as the tribe of Deukalion or the Hellenes; and finally we have the historical peoples in the proper sense, to whose ever-mounting numbers we ourselves belong.

Nevertheless, that which we have briefly alluded to as the Pelasgian race, was somehow able to transmit a meaningful portion of its influence to the generations that survived its disappearance from the historical record, and indeed traces of this unique culture have endured even unto our own generation, such as the Pelasgians' symbols, cults, myths, and other barely intelligible ritual observances. For all of the three races that we have mentioned, as well as for the prehistoric tribal groupings, the spirit is consistently regarded as being linked to a particular individual, just as we refer to a particular person's capacity for reflective cognition. However, we must now thrust this notion of reflective consciousness into the background of our discussion so that we may direct our attention to a very different type of process.

The necessity for this procedure reveals itself most clearly when we attempt to explain just what it is that we feel differentiates man from the animal, and what emerges with crystal clarity when we examine the thousandfold experiences and observations that fill the record is the obvious fact that the animal is devoid of spirit (in the precise sense in which we always employ that word). In fact, the animal organism represents the purest manifestation of the body-soul polarity to be discovered within the natural world. In utilizing the word "polarity" I am drawing attention to a process that is unrelated to the causal nexus, for neither are bodily processes the causes of psychical ones, nor are the psychical processes the causes of the bodily ones. In fact, this falsely dualistic scheme of causality was the very rock upon which Cartesian philosophy suffered its well-deserved shipwreck. There was even less truth, unfortunately, in a later theory that briefly found favor, which held, first, that the psychical (naturally confused with the spiritual!) and the body inhabit two completely discrete realms; and second, in numerous instances, a higher power introduces itself into the human organism in order to establish some type of connection between the psychical and the body. The true state of affairs is that the connection between the soul and the body is even more intimate than has ever been suspected, since nothing can transpire on the side of the body that does not coincide with an event on the side of the soul, just as no event transpires on the side of the soul without a corresponding event on the side of the body. In other words: *the body and the soul subsist in a polar connection* and the most concise formula that we can devise in order to express these relations is: *the body is the phenomenal manifestation of the soul, just as the soul is the meaning of the living body.* This can also be expressed by analogy: interpretation discloses the lexical meaning of a word, but the word is the external, or phenomenal, manifestation, of an inner meaning.

When we ponder the causal grounds whereby we have established the validity of the substrate-concept, or, to put this somewhat less technically, when we employ our critical judgment in seeking answers as to the true nature of this substrate, we must bear in mind every distinction between essences that we have drawn as well as every definition of terms that we have formulated. Now the body reveals itself in sensuous contacts and in its reaction to such contacts, and this undisputed fact alone conclusively demonstrates that the body possesses only the most tenuous of connections to the phenomenon of *distance*. The soul, on the other hand, expresses its nature in vision, which enables the bearer of soul to focus upon purposeful behavior in the furtherance of achieving certain ends, just as one's urges are obviously under the permanent sway of one's feelings.

Let us introduce an illustration which may facilitate a comprehension of these matters: the stork in Mecklenburg has no need to acquire a road-map in order to undertake the journey of thousands of kilometers that takes it back to its African habitat. *They are only following instincts*, it is often said. However, although instinct is a word that everybody employs, it is in fact a word that conceals far more than it reveals. As we proceed on our everyday round, in the course of which we recognize the world and seek to conduct our affairs within that world, we have allowed ourselves to forget that instinct has its source in an unconscious mode of recognition that regulates with absolute certainty the constitution of its bearer, just as it regulates, to some degree, every terrestrial organism; and we must, of course, include ourselves in that grouping. The foundation upon which are established the bonds connecting an unreflective reaction with a distant goal is the soul.

Let us charitably ignore the great prejudice that seems to inflate the breasts of those who believe themselves to be endowed with unique abilities due to their status as bearers of soul. However, we mentioned a moment ago that there is a not inconsiderable disadvantage connected with the nature of the animal; specifically, the incontrovertible fact that the animal's inner life is almost completely confined to its drive-impulses, just as the animal is confined to its destined environment under the constraints imposed by its evolutionary station. However, even within the soul of the animal there occurs a rudimentary collaboration between its near-sense (physical contact) and its innate capacity for far-seeing (sense of sight), just as the animal is able to make certain behavioral adjustments or accommodations in response to transformations in his environment, although some organisms, of course, are more accommodating, and hence more viable, than other organisms.

Thus, we come to realize that even the most talented of the animals possess a capacity for far-seeing that is immeasurably inferior to that of man, and the crucial distinction that has to be drawn between the animal and "primordial man" is that only man is receptive to the ever-transforming visions of spaces and times, just as he is indifferent as to whether these visions do or do not originate in his urges. In sharp contrast with the animal, his inner world is that of the far-seeing soul and not that of the narrowly constricted proximity in which bodily contacts (sense of touch) can occur. The development of this far-seeing capacity extends through the millennia, and the details as to the specifics of this development can be no more than rough approximations.

But then something utterly unprecedented transpired, for into the substance of man irrupted the lightning bolt of spirit, a daemonic force that invades man and world from a realm outside the spatio-temporal realm. The progressive development of spirit took place by incremental steps that remorselessly potentiated the hypertrophic development of goal-oriented volition in man, conscious purpose, and, finally, the will-to-business. This sinister tendency has now become a blatantly destructive will to plunder the living world.

However, at the dawn of history, and for many subsequent generations, spirit existed in a creative symbiosis with the soul. In the course of time, the balance of the poles shifted more and more towards the dominance of spirit over the soul. That development has continued all the way down to the present age. Among every people that we consider to be civilized, spirit eventually severs its ties with the soul. Grand ideas and technological discoveries have, of course, produced certain desired results; but these advances have brought a new danger in their wake. Modern man's conscious striving for power far surpasses that of any previous epoch. Today every nation is drawn deeper and deeper into this striving for dominance, without which each nation believes that it must ultimately perish. I am thinking less of the frightful wars that we must henceforth endure and more of the disturbing fact that within all peoples, this lust for power has so infected the most diverse groups that it has fastened manacles upon life itself. Woman has always been the mother and nurturer of her house, but today she sees herself so overburdened by the demands of her career that she is threatened with the forfeiture of one of her deepest missions in life, namely to serve life by becoming the guardian and protector of life and tradition.

One result of this dreadful process is that man is now in danger of losing his traditional connections with his family, just as he is endangered by the conflicts that poison the relations between employer and employee, conflicts that are interrupted by truces that have only just been declared when the rancorous hostilities erupt anew.

In the service of human needs, the ever-increasing mechanization has brought about the desecration of the natural world. Just recall how many species of wildlife have been annihilated by man during the last fifteen years alone! And, finally, we must realize that behind all of the obsessive striving for power to which we have alluded, the most gigantic—and at the same time the most destructive—is that for which we can find no more appropriate name than: *business* (in English in the original text—translator's note). While our philosophers drivel away their hours in desiccated dialectical disputations that result in nothing more significant than hairsplitting irrelevancies, money has conquered the world, and there can no longer be any doubt that the vital power whose throne has been usurped by gold, namely the soul, is now threatened by imminent destruction.

I became convinced of the validity of these perceptions many years ago, and ever since that time I have sought to communicate my findings in brief essays as well as in comprehensive treatises. However, not even the strict adherence to philosophical principles, which has forced me to proclaim the unvarnished truth about these matters to my readers, will suffice to terminate the dangerous entity that menaces the living organism, for the dreadful things that our eyes can see are but the external reflections of perilous internal transformations that are ravaging the deepest substratum of the living organism. It is precisely at this substrate level that we situate the destructive operations of that more than human power whose goal is the ultimate annihilation of the soul itself.

Goethe as Psychologist (1929)

In addition to his genius as a poet, Goethe was also a great sage whose insights into the human soul have assured him a prominent rank among the greatest psychologists in all of history. In this discussion we wish to present a coherent portrait of this man, who is alleged to have been a man whose inner life was marked by innumerable contradictions. We can best achieve our ends only after we have familiarized ourselves with the historical, as well as with the personal, context in which his unique style of thought came to fruition.

Three concepts ruled the spiritual landscape of Europe during the latter half of the eighteenth century: nature, personality, and freedom. In the Francophone sphere, of course, these elements profoundly conditioned and informed the discourse of Jean-Jacques Rousseau, and in Germany the standard-bearer of these ideas was Herder.

On one side, this constellation of ideas encouraged a love of nature, which was embodied most especially in the cult of the natural landscape; while on the other side, there developed a growing emphasis upon the emotional life of man. Thus, the "heart" reigns over the "head," just as melancholy and sensuality soon dominate mere reason and understanding.

It is this very obvious emphasis on the priority of the "heart" over the "head" that accounts for the astonishing influence exerted upon European culture by Goethe's novel *The Sorrows of Young Werther*. Likewise, this period saw a marked revival of the conviction that the vital center of the cosmos is located within the stronger personalities, a creed that was also a major component of Renaissance ideology. Once more, the loftiest development of every inherited disposition and talent within a man constituted the pinnacle of life for Europeans, just as ethical restraint and "self-discipline" began to be seen as mere hindrances and roadblocks that could only interfere with the creative unfolding of the vital powers within truly great spirits.

The young Goethe participated, of course, in the revolutionary movement that we know as the *Sturm und Drang* ("storm and stress"); nevertheless, the young Goethe soon convinced himself that there was also a danger in that chaotic indiscipline of the young disciples of the movement, a danger that might one day wreak havoc on those personalities whose inner life is not governed by the form-giving impulses that have their source in nature itself.

Thenceforth, Goethe will sing, as no one else has ever done, the melancholy side of life; in fact, all of his tragic heroes meet their downfall in the course of their struggles with destiny: Werther, Weislingen, Franz, Eduard, Ottilie, Tasso, Egmont, Faust, Gretchen, and so on.

In his own lifetime, Goethe was already hailed as the only genius who might well succeed in his mastering life-mission, which was seen as the reconciliation of elemental nature with the laws of spirit. Goethe sought to do this by harmonizing the poles of nature and spirit, unlike the procedure insisted upon by Immanuel Kant, who placed nature and spiritual law in the sharpest antithetical contrast that the mind of man could conceive.

As a personality, Goethe embodied in the most magnificent style the collaboration between the masculine, active pole and the feminine pole, characterized by a pathic receptivity. From that feminine component in his nature stems his intense feeling for actuality, just as from his masculine component stems his unprecedented ability to recognize and to reveal the sharpest critical distinctions.

A feeling for actuality and a highly developed critical sense were often treated as identical items in polite conversation during that period, although the state of affairs was quite otherwise in formal philosophical discourse. In that arena, actuality was viewed as the common possession of humanity, and one that had its source in our immediate experience, whereas the *facts,* on the other hand, are apprehended by the living person on the basis of the activity of *spirit.* Thus, as a mere fact, a stand of trees is one and the same, both when it is being gazed upon by the canny eye of the speculator who seeks to convert this segment of nature into profit or it is the living substance that forms the basis of the botanist's research. However, as an *actuality,* the stand of trees in question is perpetually renewing its phenomenal aspect, which is changed ceaselessly due to the influence of various meteorological factors, among which we will merely mention the action of the wind, and also under the shifting radiance with which the available light garbs each tree. We might even hear the claim of a landscape painter who seeks behind the immanent tree its primordial image.

Goethe's unsurpassed powers of visual discrimination led him to become the modern world's pre-eminent phenomenologist, and it may indeed be said that in Goethe we confront the essential "man of the eye."

In Goethe the operation of rational cognition transpired in harmonious accord with his feeling for the phenomenological totality. Spiritual cognition and perception of the world-image is an immediate and indivisible event, an "intuition" of fresh revelations communicated from the world without to the world within.

Whoever finds that he is able to comprehend this mode of perception and who is also able to establish his discoveries based upon the most primordial realities, will not restrict his scrutiny of life's deepest secrets to the domain of purposeful consciousness, for he is well aware of the fact that his observations are valid only while his cognitive forces have been brought into play. In fact, Goethe formulated the very concept of the unconscious, which he saw as equidistant from the pseudo-unconscious of the Leibniz school and from the verbal phantom bandied about by academic epistemologists. Goethe demonstrated that the unconscious was also not the working out of persistent physical processes within the organism that have merely eluded our notice, but rather processes that reveal themselves in talented individuals as well as in the highly trained, for the unconscious was the very foundation upon which nature erected herself, to the precise extent that nature transmits "inspiration" to the conscious mind. Goethe called this unconscious power the "daemonic," and he says of it that "every great thought that bears ripe fruit and leads to profound effects, stands far removed from the mind that would seek to control it. Man should look upon the harvested fruits of the unconscious as an unexpected windfall bestowed by Heaven above. It is our affinity with the daemonic that makes its advent seem something utterly overpowering, as it were, and often convinces an individual that this force arises from his personal impulses, whereas its primal source is actually in the unconscious substratum, a region over which, as we have seen, he exerts no control whatsoever."

In another place, Goethe asserts: "The daemonic is the force that is immune to the ministrations of rational processes. It does not always reside within my nature, although I am frequently overwhelmed by it."

At one point, Goethe goes so far along this line of speculation as to insist that the unconscious is synonymous with life itself: "Man cannot abide for very long in the conscious state; therefore man must often yield himself to the impulse that lures him ever deeper into that realm of the unconscious, for it is there that man has his deepest roots."

Far more significant than any evolutionist's conceptualization of the unconscious substrata of life is Goethe's scornful dismissal of the virtues of excessive self-observation. In the sharpest opposition to academic thought — at least as it has operated since the age of Descartes — but in consonance with the truly great psychologists of every epoch, Goethe regards the notion that we have access to immediate knowledge of the self to be a pathetic delusion: "In my opinion, man can never succeed in his attempts to know himself, since he can never install himself in the appropriate perspective from which he would be able to generate valid statements of the facts; others will always know me better than I know myself." Again: "Man can never comprehend himself with anything approaching the accuracy with which he can comprehend the world." As Goethe's readers know full well, his collected works are filled with innumerable utterances of a similar sort.

We are now able to recognize Goethe's discovery of these insights as being rooted in his unique capacity for perception. Now we turn our attention to the opposite pole, specifically of his masculine activity, for it was this orientation which irresistibly tempted him to involve himself in the active realm of public affairs, even though he retained his acuity of perception — situated at the feminine pole of his character — which never permitted Goethe to ignore (or even to forget!) that these activities (at the Weimar Court) were characterized by an almost grotesque superficiality. His watchword now is formulated in his mastering motto that claims, "To be active is man's first duty... Whenever I cannot conform myself to the demands associated with that duty, I recognize such a peculiar situation as an indication that there is a circle of endeavor to which my vocation will not grant me entrance. And I have never envisioned myself as a somnambulist." One should not too readily dismiss such utterances as expressions of Goethe's infatuation with the whole idea of the "man of action," for what is actually at work within him during these times is Goethe-as-sculptor, Goethe as a creative man whose ideal is formal excellence; what he recognized with an almost divinatory penetration was the fact that spiritual apprehension depends upon spiritual creativity! "There is no conscious experience that is not productive,

enriching, and creative." "Animals are instructed by their internal organs, said the thinkers of Antiquity, and I insist that man is himself in
precisely the same situation."

This realization introduces us now to Goethe's representation of the
"genius," one whom he regards as the bearer of a unique fund of creative
power that, in its turn, arises upon the foundation provided by the self-
renewing vitality of the genius. It is without connection to the manage-
ment of our business affairs, just as it is unrelated to our relationship with
fine art; creativity exists, in fact, quite remote from the quotidian round:
the only exceptions to this rule come into play "when our thoughts, our
connection with other people, and our deeds themselves enhance life
itself." The person to whom we apply the name "genius" demands precedence before all others with all the irresistible force of eternal youth,
for in him youth is a perpetual renewal of vitality that bursts forth like
a volcano intermittently erupting with the hot powers of perfect youth.
At such privileged moments, Goethe tells us, he experiences a "renewed
puberty." These insights were to inspire the meditations of the German
Romantics in subsequent years, and it would be the Romantics who were
able to discover new territories for psychology, although their findings,
sadly, have never been properly worked out due to the contemporary academic psychologist's superstitious faith in the all-creative power of spirit.

It is crucial to our exposition that the reader understand precisely
how significant a role Goethe's marked will-to-form played in his perception of (and reverence for) the full wealth of soul inhering in a significant human character. Likewise, Goethe was, of course, completely
justified in his recognition of the iron limits set by nature — not merely
over personal volition (a matter of quantity), but also, and perhaps more
significantly, over the idiosyncrasies of personal, "critical" judgment (a
matter of quality). No person can perceive with his senses that which
cannot be grasped by the character. "The French think precisely as they
do only because of the character with which they have been endowed."
Our own position in any meaningful ordering of rank is utterly and
completely pre-determined. It is a false belief that inspires those who
claim that the glove will always grow large enough to accommodate
one's hand satisfactorily, as we must agree if the glove in question is
crafted out of iron, for iron has an immanent shape. It is more correct to
say that the fit is determined by the inherent characteristics of the person
who is inserting his hand within the putative item. This vibrant consciousness of the iron fatality that rules our destiny is notably expressed

in the first of the "Orphic Words." Likewise, to those who erroneously believe in the (imaginary) ability of education to bring about an authentic alteration in a particular character, Goethe retorts that education is but the inculcation of rational behavior, and each student's capacity for such education is strictly governed by the talents with which he was endowed at birth. "If outstanding capacity is a pre-determined endowment, there will inevitably result the formation of an individual who is fated to achieve creative excellence in his life."

While the Romantics (and later still, Nietzsche) awaited the loftiest of life's joys in those moments when an ecstatic repression or limitation of the ego had been achieved, Goethe's own limitations were never more clearly expressed than in the quatrain in which he affirms this very limitation:

> *Commoner and prince and hero*
> *Lived and died in every age;*
> *The highest joy bestowed upon the sons of Earth*
> *Is found but in the personality.*

This attitude of Goethe's resonates quite nicely with his development of the theory of an immortal formative principle at work in nature, to which he gives the Aristotelian title of "entelechy."

Just as intimate contact with a unique life may well draw lesser mortals into its gravitational field, as it were, within which these individuals find that they actually prosper under this beneficent influence, such individuals can only be comprehended if their living context is borne in mind. The result of the process to which we refer was, in fact, the development of the Goethe-type character as it transpired in the socialized personality. To us, no one can surpass Goethe in the global treasures of richer, gentler, and nobler vitality, from which all disturbing and painful emotions have been excluded, in an ongoing synergistic potentiation of both the society as well as the individuals that comprise its components. Goethe became the most prominent apostle of good *ton* (proper social behavior — translator's note) in eighteenth century Germany, the most rigid adherent of the strictest morality that, ironically, would subsequently encourage the rise of the moralistic rabble to the stature of a significant force in history, for eventually the West's codes of law were inspired solely by a purely human conception of *Eros.*

In the end, therefore, we must avoid any suspicion that there is even a trace of irony when Goethe, in his later years, proclaims such platitudes as "The proper study of mankind is man."

On Love as *Eros* and as Passion (1922)

L et us direct our attention to certain phenomena arising from the affective stratum of life that have long been ignored by investigators. For instance, we all recognize those numerous associations that have, without exception, one interest in common, namely the employment of the group's energy to connect up with that "will to power" whose inner essence is intransigently hostile to life itself. Likewise, we have encountered those people whose connection inheres in the emotional bonds that enable individuals to participate in the sense of community that may flourish, say, in the workplace; or we may recall those ties that arise in friendly affection, as well as those bonds that are tied when sexual attraction draws two persons into more intimate connection. We finally draw attention to that which, at first glance, certainly seems to be one of the noblest attainable species of human association; namely, that intensely close union which transpires when a certain group's shared enthusiasm inspires its members to work collaboratively for the ultimate triumph of a particular enterprise, although the mission to which they have given their allegiance utterly transcends the personal, or selfish, interests of the people involved. This species of shared enthusiasm arises almost always in situations where those involved share a profound characterological affinity. Nevertheless, even this most intensely self-sacrificial form of human association, which can exist only when an ancient tribal sense of racial consciousness is intense enough to make the call of the blood potentiate the living bond of the associated persons, reveals itself, on closer scrutiny, to be dependent upon an obviously degenerate obsession with abstractions. Wherever this degenerate trend is discovered at work, as a matter of fact, the project will evolve in very short order into an entity that is soon seething with the least worthy species of partisan spirit, at which point the members become the creatures of their hollow doctrines, the most zealous missionaries preaching the most tedious ethical formalism imaginable. Utilizing the more colloquial, more "popular" lexical expression for that which had once seemed the most vital connection conceivable, we must conclude that these individuals have bogged themselves down in the phenomenon justly known as "idealism"! Since one remains protected when one stands before it, inwardly one must confess to one's belief in that which has been yearned for and anticipated in the earliest days of Eleusis, although apparently even in that place, the deepest experience could never have been brought unto its consummation: the renewal of the blood-brotherhood as it was fortified within the bearer of the mystery of *Eros.*

Suppose one were sought out by a person who wished to question us as to our personal recollections of a visionary revelation to which we happened to have been an eyewitness (in order to acquire additional details about the scene) — if, suddenly, we should learn there was a second witness to that very vision, we are bound by that event in a sympathetic connection with that other person. To that connection, we give the name of the cosmogonic *Eros*! That such an event has nothing to do with the physical expression of bodies goes without saying; but it may, however, come to pass that such an inoffensive connection might well result in a person's experience of so transformative a miracle that he feels himself transported among the gods. Events about which no one hears since they happened to have transpired between two individuals out of hundreds of millions, might actually break the fleeting power of the spirit, the destructive nightmare of "world history" might be shattered, and we might awaken in a world "blossoming with streams of light."

We wish now to clarify, in a few brief words, just what it is that inheres in the notion of a love that is "faithful beyond death," a species of passion, as it happens, about which the ancient world knew precisely nothing. The Epoptes, in fact, regarded the very condition of "bodiliness" as a potent symbol that enabled man to participate in the stream of images that constitutes the soul of the world. Let us consider the case of one who is not "merely" loved, but rather that of the person whose innermost passion is to possess another utterly and to the deepest levels of that person's life — we might recall Solveig's love for Peer (Gynt — translator's note) — he is necessarily viewing the object of his obsessive passion as if through a fog that renders his gaze identical in essence with the eye of the "world-creating" God, before whom the sur-face of the Earth is pulverized as the mortal coil of the flesh begins to glow with the penetrating radiance of the elemental soul. As if he were truly becoming a man on fire, he probes the humanity of his beloved, but with the ray of light that reveals merely the presence of his own de-mon. In this case—whose lineaments are common to the vision of *Eros* that was characteristic not only of Greek Antiquity but of the Germanic Middle Ages as well—it is nonetheless only to state that this standpoint did not exclude the possibility that a magical image might transmit its reflections while the image wandered from person to person. The least enduring experience of an erotic connection in itself cannot keep pace with the most fulfilling inwardness, and it is precisely in the midst of the most freely bestowed and most overflowing sexual experience that, without the slightest contradiction, transpires the payment of money to a member of the class of *hetairas*...

Ever more constricting, however, becomes this passion now that his ego consumes the object of love with its soul, until the nature of the "character" of the person so obsessed with this passion-as-exclusivity be-comes more and more rigid and unyielding, so that in time there may even arise a serious danger that the lightning bolt of vision itself becomes increasingly constricted, until the only thing on the lover's mind is the tormenting riddle of an individual's personality. The person severs his vital bonds with the sensuous world of images, all of which are stripped away until the human being believes that the beloved has become a god to be worshipped in the place of a god. This mode of passion has now obviously metamorphosed into idolatry, and with its advent begins the ultimate tragedy of *Eros*. Whereas once the lovers were filled with rap-ture when they formed one interfused flame of vital imagery, the person now seeks the essence of love in the human "self" of the beloved, so that he may raise his beloved to the stature of a spiritual being whom he seizes fast in the dimension of duration, whereas only in the releasing of the beloved from all such chains may he live an eternity in an instant of time. Thus there transpires the pathos of a "grand passion," which constrains the lover to secure for himself that passionate "loyalty unto death," which even seeks to extend its domain beyond the borders of the tomb, and which, scrutinized from the standpoint of metaphysics, can only, and always, result in misfortune for both persons. Then, inevita-bly, the lover is demanding the pseudo-fulfillment of his passion as he commands that he be granted the sole access to the body of his beloved, so that, sooner or later, disaster occurs (Faust and Gretchen!); but no matter how much the lover torments her, betrays her, ridicules her, this same lover swears that he would, without hesitation, give up his life for his beloved; nevertheless, no matter how heroic is the deed of the martyr, by itself the martyrdom avails him nothing in the face of all-powerful death! In every modality in which we encounter the "love unto God" there is always present a very deep share in the sacrament of *Eros*; but in the "grand passion" there is always an impulsive undercurrent that is seeking to build a bridge to the faith in immortality: whatever wishes of ours cannot attain to fulfillment "here" must be fulfilled to the limit of our hopes in the transcendent "yonder."

However, "immortality" is only a pathological yearning for the ful-fillment of unfulfillable wishes, and the entire history of our cosmos, in comparison with which the whole chronicle of mankind is merely a drop in the ocean of time, cries unrelentingly that even the beloved is doomed to be a thing of corruption and dissolution. The nimbus sur-rounding that wish, whose loftiness is perpetually rewoven — and quite righly so — should not, however, blind us to the fact that this is a wish that life cannot fulfill without dissolving that self to nothingness in the very process.

And now we turn back from the melancholy image of the tormented greatness of man to the breathing brightness of the world of gods, as they once promised the following to the poet:

What fiery wonder transpires when the waves transfigure us,
As they shatter, one upon the other, in their coruscating radiance?
They glow and shift and shimmer ever onwards:
And the stars and planets are gleaming on their nocturnal paths,
And everything is ringed around by the fire;
This is the all-ruling Eros, *begetter of everything that lives!*

The Identity of Spirit in Every Bearer of Life (1920)

When I comprehend an existing thing, I am compelled to negate by means of a process of abstraction: first, the temporal dimension of that which is experienced; second, the spatial dimension of that which is experienced; and third, the uniqueness of that which is experienced.

One bearer of life is distinguished from all other bearers of life through the personal nature of that which is experienced; in other words, through the spatio-temporal uniqueness of that experience. If, however, the realization of this truth should evade one's notice, then a particular discovery must necessarily be regarded as the self-same entity as it appears in different epochs as well as its appearance for various discoverers. Thus, when several individuals believe that they have perceived the self-same thing, they are, in fact, ignoring the vital fact that their sensory experiences are uniquely personal and therefore, one person's experience is distinct from that of any other person. On the other hand, there must also be revealed in every single pondered moment of life and within all bearers of life the self-same disposition (*Anlage*), by whose agency the act of understanding is consummated. We designate that agent, considered in itself and for itself, with the name spirit, and in our consideration of its manifestation within an individual person's living nature, we call it the ego. The justification for our choice of the name "spirit" is the result of simple reflection, especially when the discussion turns to scrutinize the faculty of judgment, which at the very least is indubitably a creature of the spirit. The justification of the name "ego" is founded upon the circumstance that every judgment necessitates a critically judging ego in order to be able to arrive at that judgment. I judge, as follows: here stands a tree, therefore I can judge: I judge that here is standing a tree; and so it goes through every conceivable case.

However, if the relation of the ego to the living organism transpires according to the disposition of the critically judging ego, and the critically judging ego acts in the living organism solely according to the activity of the spirit, then the spirit must be identical in every person. Therefore, spirit's determinations are necessarily binding upon every formulation of a correct judgment, as well as for every individual "without distinction of person" in his capacity as one who formulates critical judgments. And here again the ego is the self-same entity throughout every segment of a person's constitution; accordingly, it is demonstrably true that in every statement of the following type: I performed this or that deed, "then," shall we say, approximately fifteen years previously — both one's experience as well as one's experienced physicality was completely different from one's present experience and its physicality. Just as outside the "thing-point" there is a living self, there is *within* each person the "ego-point." We refer to the ego as the "manifestation" of spirit within the realm of life, just as we designate the thing as the "projection" of the ego into the sphere of actuality. Both things and egos are quantifiable; and that which we customarily quantify, we quantify with reference to them.

As soon as we have grasped these principles, we will likewise comprehend: it is the essence of the thing that it can never constitute an actuality that is independent of consciousness. The sole unconditioned actualities are the images...

The Poems

In the Distant West

The sun descends the western skies.
It flames and flares far in the west,
And heaven, in that far-flung west,
Gleams clear and bright as crystal.
Blue, so blue, the deepest distance
    Now intoxicates my senses,
    Till my soul is trembling, reeling,
    Sundered by a sudden yearning.
    Beams of light assail my eyes:
They press against the moistened lashes,
    Forcing out, with sudden instancy,
        One unaccustomed tear.

The Herd

O muffled echo of the bells. A shepherd
    Leads his flock from off the hill.
Uncanny: from behind the woods, the west'ring sun
    Shoots spears of flame through seas of mist.

    Soon awkward gloaming abdicates,
    And wilder weather takes the skies.
But where is now the flock, and where its shepherd?
    Then — the rage of thunder in the night.

137

RUNES

We've not the slightest yearning for the social world:
The storms and omens of the Cosmos will suffice.

REVERBERATION

Evening's chill blows softly from the hills;
The sun declines towards the tree-tops.
From the shadowed valleys all sounds perish.
Bitter yearning! Giant clouds glide down the sky,
As night, in mourning garb, enshrouds a deeper sorrow
Under ebon wings.

THE STREAM

Into the silence of the night,
There breaks the rushing, splashing stream;
Upon the purling waters
Breezes gently blow
And silver moonbeams dance.

Now wind-bowed poplars
Brew a sleepy potion in the depths.
Throughout the trees roar stabbing winds,
Until the swirling burden of the fallen leaves
At last can still the raging waters.

RUNES

Massive and oppressive dome of heaven —
Timid glimmer from the cloudy vault —
O dark, close-woven web of night…

The deep-resounding clangor of the bells —
There lingers now in evening's red,
And on the lofty battlements, a final gleam…

A groan emerges from the darkling woods.
The fog is near — the world is far.

THE EVENING OF LIFE

The evening of my life is fading fast,
And on the long, dour street are cast —
In yellow gleam of candelabra —
Shapes long lost in time.
The melancholy and the misery of things…

SONG

And if it really was a dream,
Why should one suffer so?
As storm-winds roared,
The welkin raged
From sea to sea to sea;
And all the while
The evening sun shed
Wretched rags of light.
We die, and are forgotten,
Even by the grandsons
Strolling on our graves.

And if it really was a dream,
Why should one suffer so?
The storms are roaring,
And above the lands
The gloomy clouds sail on.
Whole nations die, and are forgotten,
And above the wreckage
Time prepares the entry
Of the coming generation.

And if it really was a dream,
Why should one suffer so?
The storm-wind screams,
The welkin shrieks;
The very stars will die
And be forgotten.
Still, there'll always be
Some novel bloom, which,
Nourished by the dust of the deceased,
Will one day wander far
On bright, celestial paths.

· ⚡—◆❯◯❮◆—⚡ ·

WINDY FIELD

A damned soul, stripped by death, adorns
The ravaged field; tormented grasses moan.
The atmosphere soon fades to black,
As storm-winds wail in devastated forests.

Eyes stare, almost blinded, through the raging floods.
The night is raucous in its clamor.
Night looms high above your pallid captain—
Viking long-boats sail into the Nordic distance.

· ⚡—◆❯◯❮◆—⚡ ·

MELANCHOLY MORNING

It is a colder, sadder morning;
Brazen clouds hang high up in the heavens;
There they want to stay. No rain is falling;
Not a breeze disturbs the rigid hedgerows.

Morbid thoughts upon awakening…
As memories assume command,
The soul grows pale, its contours quake,
As if beneath a mountain made of steel and ice.

O night, break through! O sleep, descend!
Drown knowledge in a blacker flood!
From dream-tormented torture chambers,
Rouse yourself and radiate your eerie light.

EVENING

At last the raging forces tremble;
Growing weary, soon they'll slumber.
Storm-winds fade, and everywhere
Is night, so black, so cold.

The darkly massive clouds are surging,
Sleeping through the humid night.
Now here, now there, on heaven's dome
A gentle star turns on its lamp.

Like buried slag aglow once more
When stirred to life by vagrant gusts,
My deep regrets take hold of me
When distant clocks toll out the hours.

Be still, my heart! Breathe easily;
The feeble clangor has been stilled,

And stars are shining silently
Above the quiet woods.

AS THE CANDLES FLICKER

The candles flicker. Midnight bellows
From the tower. As the storm
Goes rooting through the night,
It roars with laughter.
Tremble—you are but an atom
Shot into the raging flux,
Wherein the ages whirl and toss
Forever.

PHILOSOPHY

Of what avail is all philosophy?
We'll never solve the riddle of existence.
In the end, look where you will, our thought
Is nothing but a game we play with words.

LIFE

Hectic movement, harried haste—
No time to pause, no chance to rest—
A warm embrace, a fervent kiss—
And then divorce and flight afar—
Divorce, detest, and reconcile—
And then split up again—
That's life! Yes, that is life.

It babbles in the rains; it riots in the clouds;
It flutters in the leaves, and sighs in winds of storm—
And all *will be, is* now, or *was*—
And all once *was* and *will return*—
As, without cease, life spins its whirling fabric
Through eternal aeons.

Gone forever—like the waves upon the shoreline—
Gone forever! Gone, but whence? And whither?
Life knows not the waves; it only knows the *sea*.
Life only knows the sea and will remain eternal and complete.
And yet it is the sun-glossed *waves* that murmur
As they storm the sandy shore.

EVENING SONG

Into the west, the distant west!
For that is where I long to be;
And if the clouds above were little skiffs,
They would descend and bear me off
On wondrous paths, towards
The purple-glowing sun
Within the distant west!

Is there a land, is there a life,
Where magic, flaming colors
Spark such scintillant reflections
On the gleaming waters?
Do you know? And nor do I!
Could Earth afford a rapture more profound
Than that which floods the heart
When our world sinks and dives
Into those flaming, sparkling seas?
Into the west, the distant west!

I must go forth, I must depart!
The sun is sinking, now it's gone.
My eyes but stare forlorn
Towards the fiery seas.
My yearning swells, I breathe so deeply
As the darkness grows apace.
But solar splendor still irradiates
The distant cloud-bank:
Westward ho!

AWAKEN

You awaken still within me,
Boundless cosmic soul!
And yet you hesitate, at first,
To loose me from the murk
Of mortal slumbers:
Then I am dissolved into
A million shining atoms;
Now the dull gray spider
Of deceit o'er-shadows all!
And still you would alert me,
For the onset of my madness is at hand.

I'm helpless,
For the demon ego
Locks me in the dungeon
Of the day's dim dream.
O sorrow, sorrow! Into lightless depths
You tumble downwards, cosmic soul!
The shadow of the ego thrashes wildly,
As it bursts forth from Lethean waters.
Hearken to the rush and roar!
The lying mask of life
Erupts into the holy darkness,
And the feeble rays of dawn are weaving now

Deceiving webs of being!
Now my ear can tell the sighing
Of the cold winds through the tree-tops
From the crowing of the cock.

O cosmic soul, you plunge me
Into fatal slumbers, whirling me about
Within the frenzied waves.
Once more, I am condemned
To think the mad thought of existence,
Whilst I struggle like some banished being
In the storm-erected tidal waves
Of ancient strife.

YULETIDE

As wilding winds wail through bare branches,
Storm-clouds shroud with gloom the hours.
But soon our weary world is blessed; she sips
From glossy goblet sweet forgetfulness...

The saviour's name and nature maze and mystify,
So potent is the precious potion;
And then the arctic nocturne yields
Unto a glowing reverie of perfumed, rose-rich lands,

Where we watch wide-eyed as the kindled torches
Swift illumes a realm wherein the orphan knows no peril —
Spirit has no strength to bind our wings;
No wheezing whirlwind can impede our flight.

All's well! Spill forth now, cataracts of light,
Shine on imperiously, irradiated whirlwinds:
For we who shimmer with life's incandescence,
Fear no pale ghost spawned in fever-swamps of madness.

BIRTH

O gloomy night—
O night high-vaulted—
What uproots these winter-knotted trees?
Through heaven's cove
The predator is on the spoor,
And foam flies from the neighing chargers.

Gaping night—
Bright-glowing night—
A dazzling gleam lights up black hilltops.
Flickering and twisting—
Coldly sparkling—
Stars are shattered in a night of storm.

And time is rolling onwards,
Rumbling, roaring—
Hurricanes assail high crag and sodden woodland.
Cautious cries creep forth
From smoky trees,
And then drift to the heights
Where eagles sit on brood.

LULLABY

Listen to the splashing rain
That purls and pours upon the roof.
O sleep, beloved child of mine,
Though howling storms sweep high
Above our twilit homeland.
Listen as the clock ticks out
The minutes and the seconds—

As the night is fading fast away
And dawn's light adumbrates the day,
So too do you approach a life of sorrow now
With every step that you will take.
Yet sleep awhile, sleep long, beloved child.

Are you asleep, O heart of mine?
Or do you listen to the pouring, purling rain?
Attend to these great storm-winds whistling
All around our safe and solid home.
You do not know that all these tears of heaven
Signify but care and sorrow,
For with moaning and with lamentation
All the seconds of your life will throb:
Their shafts are aimed right at your heart,
To spill your scarlet blood in endless streams.
O hearken! Through the roaring storm
The watchman on the tower blows the warning blast.
How swiftly midnight comes to call.
But sleep, my little one: your mother shall stand guard!

MAN AND HIS GOD

Into uncanny loneliness
We're one and all expelled
From nowhere.
Yet within each mortal
Dwells his god.
The world must always master man:
But help me conquer loneliness!
That's all I ask of you, of you my god!

REMEMBRANCE, DARKLING

In my darkest depths, the atom clouds
Recall a dreamily unconscious era,
When they rested in the hearts
Of flowers of the fields.
They yearn for swift release
Into the stream of life,
Once more to flood the world with sweet aromas —
Where they might ban utterly
All fraudulent display,
Companioned by most secret consubstantial powers,
Scattering their congregated throng unto
The infinite celestial vault.
And that which, deep within me,
Yet participates in waves ethereal
Hath intermingled with the heaven's blue.
The earthly portion yet residing in my frame,
Is incarnated as a clotted mist
That blots all distance out;
And what has most intensely pulsed
And throbbed within me
Shrieks and hisses like great leaping flares
Upon the surface of the sun.

THE CLUTCHING TALONS

When I recall you, silent nature,
Deep within me magic pictures coalesce;
And that which rules me from without,
The merely melancholy satisfaction of my longing,
Lures me on to follow to the end
The dark, enduring traces of a world
That fades to nothingness whilst yet I gaze.
But is it just my own desire
That splits my heart in twain?

Two stressors drive the creature netherwards:
The one will drag him down
Into a boundless waste of dust;
The other rolls and tumbles him unto the void.
And carnal pleasure — as it will be, not as it is now! —
Disintegrates the creature's form.
Yet that which liberates, evokes no will in him
To brave the raging of the storms.
Instead, the creature merely craves
The clutching talons that imprison him.

MAN AND DOG AND BIRD

The rabid mongrel rotates in tight circles,
Straining to devour the raven.
Yet the cur achieves no purchase on the wings,
And all that's left him is a hollow boast.

The clumsy wretch is waterlogged without
And hot with rage within:
Since he himself can't fly at all,
His envy roasts his soul alive.

We humans also saw the bird,
Although we did not crave its wings.
We know: whatever soars so high above
Must ultimately crash into the dust.

The art of flight has also left us listless;
But the thought of our mortality
Comes in a blinding flash
As buckshot blasts the bird apart.

THE GENIUS

Danger lurks within the surges
That divide him from the island of the yet unborn,
Till breakers toss him down upon
The ragged coastline of a storm-tossed realm.
The lamentation of the waves
Dissolves into the powdered stones.

Alone with his great love,
Not knowing his true name or nature,
He must prowl dark roads;
Must gaze upon bright-burning deserts
And at shadow-shedding welkin high above;
Must stand amid the strafing whirlwind
Whilst his love is stunned,
Constrained by outer darkness,
And his life's own inner fire incinerates
The noontide of his days.

But where his flawless flame extends,
All distances are glossed with gold;
And every dull gray land of storm
Is soon made lustrous at the sound
Of his tormented song.

Index

Y

Z

Other titles published by Arktos:

Beyond Human Rights
by Alain de Benoist

Manifesto for a European Renaissance
by Alain de Benoist & Charles Champetier

The Problem of Democracy
by Alain de Benoist

Germany's Third Empire
by Arthur Moeller van den Bruck

The Arctic Home in the Vedas
by Bal Gangadhar Tilak

Revolution from Above
by Kerry Bolton

The Fourth Political Theory
by Alexander Dugin

Fascism Viewed from the Right
by Julius Evola

Metaphysics of War
by Julius Evola

The Path of Cinnabar
by Julius Evola

Archeofuturism
by Guillaume Faye

Convergence of Catastrophes
by Guillaume Faye

Why We Fight
by Guillaume Faye

The WASP Question
by Andrew Fraser

War and Democracy
by Paul Gottfried

The Saga of the Aryan Race
by Porus Homi Havewala

Homo Maximus
by Lars Holger Holm

The Owls of Afrasiab
by Lars Holger Holm

De Naturae Natura
by Alexander Jacob

Fighting for the Essence
by Pierre Krebs

Can Life Prevail?
by Pentti Linkola

Guillaume Faye and the Battle of Europe
by Michael O'Meara

The Ten Commandments of Propaganda
by Brian Anse Patrick

A Handbook of Traditional Living
by Raido

The Agni and the Ecstasy
by Steven J. Rosen

The Jedi in the Lotus
by Steven J. Rosen

It Cannot Be Stormed
by Ernst von Salomon

Tradition & Revolution
by Troy Southgate

Against Democracy and Equality
by Tomislav Sunic

The Initiate: Journal of Traditional Studies
by David J. Wingfield (ed.)

9 781907 166617